MAINE'S GREATEST ATHLETES

Nancy Griffin

Camden, Maine

Down East Books

An imprint of The Rowman & Littlefield Publishing Group, Inc.
4501 Forbes Blvd., Ste. 200
Lanham, MD 20706
www.rowman.com

Distributed by NATIONAL BOOK NETWORK

British Library Cataloguing in Publication Information available

Library of Congress Cataloging-in-Publication Data available

ISBN 978-1-60893-740-0 (paper : alk. paper)
ISBN 978-1-60893-741-7 (electronic)

♾™ The paper used in this publication meets the minimum requirements of American National Standard for Information Sciences—Permanence of Paper for Printed Library Materials, ANSI/NISO Z39.48-1992.

This book is dedicated to my youngest grandchildren,
Matthew and Meara Van Der Zee,
and to every kid in Maine with a dream.
May you achieve those dreams.

CONTENTS

FOREWORD

Sports have long been recognized as a way for poor urban youth to make it out of poverty. For instance, traditionally, the best boxers in a city often emerge from the latest round of immigrants. Along with boxing, running, baseball, and basketball are other sports that require little equipment or infrastructure, giving blue-collar kids a better shot at success.

In the state of Maine, with its tiny population, its rural and low-income nature, cities that barely count as towns in more populous states, and its distance from major urban centers where success may be easier to attain, achieving success meant athletes had to be better, work harder, and, if they actually reached the heights, in some cases did it when they were older than their urban competitors. Many truly talented athletes from all disciplines never made the big time, because luck also counts when so many factors are working against athletic success.

Back in 1790, around the time the earliest athletes featured in this book were born, the population of Maine was a mere 96,540 people. Today it is still only 1,338,404. So, while the number of truly famous athletes in this book is few, they are drawn from a tiny number of determined people. In the book, we feature 50 athletes who achieved a great measure of success and perhaps fame despite the odds.

A few of the outstanding athletes featured here came from families in which many members were similarly talented, although not always in the same sport. Certainly not every athlete in the book came from poverty, either. They are a varied group drawn from different sports, genders, ethnic backgrounds and socio-economic levels. But they all share three things: talent, passion, and a strong connection to the State of Maine.

1

JOAN BENOIT SAMUELSON

Number One in So Many Ways

In the firmament of Maine athletes, runner Joan Benoit Samuelson is likely the best known star, especially in contemporary terms, since she was the winner of the world's first Women's Olympic Marathon in 1984 and her record of 2:24:52 still holds. Her time, 2:22:43, for winning the 1983 Boston Marathon held the course record for 11 years. She also won the Chicago marathon in 1983, setting a world record for an American woman with 2:21:21 that held for 18 years, and a course record that held for 32 years.

Benoit's parents were skiers who encouraged athleticism in their four children. The diminutive Joan did not start running until she was 15, and then only to aid in her recovery from a broken leg suffered while slalom skiing. Turned out she had quite a knack for it.

Born Joan Benoit on May 16, 1957, in Cape Elizabeth, Maine, she always excelled at sports, but running replaced all the others soon after she took it up. She joined the new girls' track team at her high school in 1972 and quickly became its star. Despite little support for female runners at the time, she began training on her own to run a future marathon, often logging 200 miles a week.

She left Bowdoin College in 1977 for a running scholarship at North Carolina State, earning All-America titles there in 1977 and 1978 and leading her school to an Atlantic Coast Conference cross-country championship. She returned to Bowdoin to complete her degree in history and environmental studies in 1979 and entered the Boston Marathon the same year. One of the oldest marathons in the country, run continuously since 1897, the Boston race banned women until 1972.

The 5'3", 105-pound Benoit sported a Boston Red Sox baseball cap during that first Boston Marathon race. She may have been the only runner who first performed a two-mile sprint to reach the Hopkinton starting line after being stuck in traffic. A virtual unknown at the time, she beat the record by eight minutes, coming in at 2:35:15.

After a severe knee injury and surgery in 1984, her chances for the first Olympic Women's Marathon looked chancy. However, she recovered faster than expected and won the trials. Three months later, she made history. The same year, she won the Jessie Owens Award and was named the Women's Sports Foundation Amateur Sportswoman of the year, Subsequent injuries slowed her running career, but she was awarded the James E. Sullivan Award in 1985 as the country's top amateur athlete.

The international superstar put her hometown of Cape Elizabeth on the map for elite runners when she founded the Beach to Beacon 10k Road Race in 1998, a 6.2-mile race held every August that starts at Crescent Beach State Park and goes to Fort Williams Park and Portland Head Light.

"A long-time dream of mine has been realized" said Benoit Samuelson. "I've always wanted to create a race that brings runners to some of my most favorite training grounds, so that they can enjoy the same beautiful environment, sense of community and rich history that has played such an important role in my life." Winners of the race have hailed from as far away as Ethiopia, Kenya, the UK, Mexico and more. She has used her fame to help charities that include the Special Olympics, Multiple Sclerosis and Big Sisters of Boston. She's

Benoit Samuelson, recognized simply as "Joanie" in Maine, also placed first in her age group in the Boston Marathon in 2011, finishing in 2:51:29. She also completed many other marathons as far away as New Zealand, including setting an over-50 division record with 2:49:09 in the 2009 New York City marathon. She was inducted into the Maine Women's Hall of Fame in 2000.

Marathons were not her only racing successes. She won the prestigious 7.1 mile Falmouth (Massachusetts) Road Race six times in 1976, 1978, 1981, 1982, 1983 and 1985, breaking the course record four times.

Benoit married her college sweetheart, Scott Samuelson in 1984. They live in Freeport, where the high school athletic complex is named for her. The Samuelsons have two children, a daughter, Abigail (Abby) and a son, Anders, both runners. When Joan ran the 1987 Boston Marathon, she was three months pregnant and finished second. In 2014, she ran the Boston Marathon with both of her children.

"Joanie" might be Maine's busiest person. She gardens. She's an author. She goes on ski trips with her husband and kids. She wrote her biography, "Running Tide" with Sally Baker, and "Running for Women" with Gloria Overmuch. She is a motivational speaker. She opened a running clinic. She is a sports commentator. She coaches cross-country and long-distance runners. Nike has designed a line of shoes inspired by her winning the first Women's Olympic Marathon in 1984. Her voice is featured on the company's Nike + iPod system as a congratulatory voice.

Nike lauds Benoit Samuelson this way: "In two hours, 24 minutes and 52 seconds, Joan Benoit Samuelson ignited a revolution. The year was 1984, the location: Los Angeles, the event: the first women's marathon in the history of the Games. The victory definitively decimated obsolete notions that had previously limited women's running to 1,500 meters: the belief that women weren't physically capable of enduring such distances."

All these accomplishments might be enough for another athlete, but Benoit Samuelson isn't just any other athlete. In 2019, she once again entered the Boston Marathon, 40 years after her record-setting victory there. As they had in previous marathons, she and daughter Abby ran together. "Joanie" hoped to celebrate the anniversary by coming in within 40 minutes of her historic time of 2:35:15.

However, at age 61, she bested her goal by coming in within 30 minutes of that time, at 3:04. She's not just an athlete and a superstar, she's someone who has genuinely earned the title of legend.

2

EDMUND "RIP" BLACK

From Hauling Traps to Throwing the Hammer

Edmund "Rip" Black grew up on Bailey's Island, Maine, and early on practiced the profession of many islanders—lobster fishing. In fact, despite achieving high honors in all his high school's sports, family and friends had to convince him to go to college instead of going straight to pulling traps.

Eventually he was persuaded. He graduated Portland High, where he played baseball and hockey, captained the track and field squads, and was named the state's best high school fullback in 1923. But still he didn't go on to college immediately. He spent two years after graduation lobstering.

Finally, he headed to the University of Maine in Orono, where once again he showed his prowess in several sports by playing football and baseball. He threw a no-hitter against the Bowdoin College team in 1927. But at Orono he discovered the hammer throw.

Black proved so good at the hammer throw that he entered the Olympic trials at Harvard Stadium in Cambridge, Massachusetts, in 1928. He won. The next step was a trip to the Summer Olympics in Amsterdam aboard the SS *Roosevelt*. Considered the best chance for the United States to bring home a medal in the event, Black didn't fail.

He came home to Maine having won the bronze medal with a throw of 160 feet, 10½ inches.

He didn't qualify for the 1932 Olympics in Los Angeles so he dropped the hammer and returned to his first love: lobstering. He worked as a lobster buyer for a few years, but began fishing and stuck with it until he retired at age 85.

His son, Bill, said lobstering suited his father's independent spirit, and that hauling with his dad for ten hours a day instilled in him a great work ethic.

Like any good athlete, Black couldn't sit around when lobstering died down in the winter. He took up candlepin bowling and true to form, he excelled. He reportedly played 50 games in one day.

Black lived from May 3, 1905, to October 22, 1996. He suffered from Alzheimer's disease in later years, and moved to Westboro, Massachusetts, with his son in 1993, where he later died from complications of pneumonia.

3

CINDY BLODGETT

Among America's Top Female Basketball Players

Cindy Lee Blodgett is Maine's all-time leading scorer for high school basketball, led the University of Maine (UMO) to its first four NCAA Tournament appearances, still holds at least 18 school records, and is ranked sixth in NCAA scoring history. One sportswriter called her "one of the greatest athletes in New England history."

Blodgett was born in the small town of Clinton in a rural area of Maine on December 23, 1975. When she was little, her father found an old pipe, stuck it in their driveway, welded a hoop to it, and launched his daughter's basketball career.

She attended Lawrence High School, leading her Bulldogs team to four Class A state championships with a record of 84–4. She is still Maine's top high school basketball scorer with 2,596 points.

A high school coach remembered her as dedicated and tough, recalling when she split her head open in a collision during a semifinal game, but returned to the game to score 19 more points.

Her stellar statistics brought her offers from large schools such as Notre Dame and the University of Colorado, but she turned them down to stay in Maine.

Before she attended UMO, two biographies had been written about her, one by Tabitha King, wife of Stephen King. Both had graduated from Orono and ended up attending all the games. The women' team often outdrew the popular men's hockey team.

At the University of Maine, she led the Black Bears to their first four NCAA tournaments, scoring a record 3,005 points in her college career—a record she still holds. She was only the second woman to lead the country in scoring for four consecutive college seasons.

A 60–58 victory in 1999 remains the only NCAA tournament victory, men's or women's, in Black Bear history.

She also earned two America East Player-of-the-Year awards, four WBCA District I All-America honors, four America East Tournament MVP awards, and was chosen three times as an ECAC Division All-Star.

After graduating UMO cum laude with a BS in elementary education in 1998, she was a first-round pick for the Women's National Basketball Association (WNBA) Cleveland Rockers team. She played there for one year, then joined the Sacramento Monarchs. She also played for the Springfield Spirit and in Korea and France.

Blodgett's first coaching job was as an assistant coach at Boston University in 1999, followed by the same position at Brown University in Rhode Island. She returned to her alma mater in 2007 when she was named head women's basketball coach at the University of Maine. Four years later, she moved to the University of Rhode Island as an assistant coach, then to Boston University again.

In 2018 she left the world of collegiate coaching after 16 years to serve as head varsity basketball coach for the Lincoln School, a private girls' prep school in Providence, Rhode Island.

A four-time All-American during her 1994–1998 University of Maine career, she was inducted into the Maine Basketball Hall of Fame in 2018, the University of Maine Hall of Fame in 2003, and the Maine Sports Hall of Fame in 2009.

Beloved in Maine and her hometown, she returned to Clinton in 2005 to attend the dedication of Cindy Blodgett Park, an outdoor basketball court partly funded by another Maine legend, Stephen King, through the Stephen and Tabitha King Foundation.

"I grew up playing at home, in my driveway. My dad welded together a hoop and I just pounded it and pounded it all day and all night," said Blodgett at the dedication. "Something like this, an actual park and a court, is just awesome for today's kids."

4

DANNY BOLDUC

Maine's First Hockey Olympian and NHL Player

Daniel "Danny" Bolduc was born in Waterville, May 6, 1953. He wasted no time starting on his hockey career when he was nine years old by being named most valuable player (MVP) in the pee wee hockey national tournament two years in a row for his division. The second year win, when he was ten, included 7 goals in one game and 20 for the tournament.

His freshman year at Waterville High, he led the Panthers to the New England Hockey Championship. For his junior year, he transferred to Phillips Andover Academy where he quickly established a scoring record and was named Prep All-American. He also served as team captain in 1971 and 1972.

After high school, Bolduc attended Harvard University where the Crimsons made it to the Frozen Four national college championships twice. For the Crimsons, the left-wing Bolduc set team and New England records for the number of goals scored in a short time. Although elected captain of the team for his senior year, he chose instead to join the U.S. team for the 1976 Winter Olympics in Innsbruck, Austria, making him the first hockey player from Maine to compete in the Olympics. He scored two goals and said it was "the thrill of a lifetime."

Following college and the Olympics, Bolduc began his decade-long professional hockey career with the New England Whalers of the World Hockey Association. Two years later he played for the United States in the 1976 Canada Cup and the 1979 Ice Hockey World Championship.

Bolduc became the first Mainer to play for the National Hockey League (NHL) when he joined the Detroit Red Wings in 1978. He also played for the NHL's Calgary Flames and a number of AHL teams, and was named AHL Calder Cup Champion 1980–1981.

He is married to Rebecca "Becky" Mitchell, also of Waterville, whose father, John "Swisher" Mitchell, was a noted Maine athlete himself. Like his son-in-law, Mitchell was an inductee into the Maine Sports Hall of Fame, among others, as a basketball star. He was also the beloved assistant basketball coach at Colby College for 40 years.

Bolduc was inducted into the Maine Sports Hall of Fame in 1981 and retired from pro hockey in 1985, with an NHL record of 41 points in a 102-game career. Although his education and hockey career took him to many places, he always returned to Maine and resides on Messalonskee Lake in a home he and his wife built in 1980. At age 65, he began a new career, working as director of the Maine Bureau of Labor Standards.

"I feel that the state of Maine laid a solid foundation for me to build a dream life and what a pleasant ride it has been."

5

MIKE BORDICK

Major League Shortstop Record Holder

Michael Todd "Mike" Bordick, was not born in Maine, but because the family moved around with his Air Force father, he spent some of his childhood there; then they returned to settle in Winterport when Mike was a sophomore in high school. He was born July 21, 1965, in Marquette, Michigan.

As a member of the Hampden Academy Broncos baseball team, Bordick was a star. His dad, also Mike Bordick, was a beloved kids' baseball coach in town. Being in a state where the warm season is short, Hampden Academy played only 12 baseball games a year, so teams rarely attracted college scouts. Players would start practice indoors in the gym in February or March, and move outdoors often while the ground was still frozen. At Hampden, he also played football and basketball. A classmate was NASCAR driver Ricky Craven.

Bordick said learning to play in Maine with the short season was beneficial: "If there was a day that you could put a jacket on and it wasn't snowing, we'd be outside playing baseball."

He went on to the University of Maine in Orono, where he played shortstop for three seasons that included two trips to the College World Series in 1984 and 1986. Bordick batted .296 for his college career and .364 during his junior year. His team set a Maine record,

61, for double plays and made All-New England and All-Northeast Regional Tournament.

In 1986, Bordick's junior year, a scout from the Oakland Athletics watched him play and thought the 5-foot, 10-inch, 160-lb infielder had a special quality. J. P. Ricciardi put Bordick 15th on a list of 25 potential draft choices, but Bordick wasn't eager to leave school. That summer Bordick played in the Cape Cod League for the Yarmouth-Dennis Red Sox and Ricciardi offered him a bonus to join the A's as an amateur free agent. Bordick accepted and began his 13 years in major league baseball.

First he asked his dad whether he should drop out of school for the offer, and his dad said, "You can go to school and finish up any time . . . but you only have one shot at this. This is your dream . . . and a lot of people don't have their dream come true."

By 1990, he was a full-fledged member of the A's. A former Oakland teammate, Billy Beane, said of Bordick, "If you could ever create the sort of player you'd want in the clubhouse and on the field, how he carries himself, he's the guy who'd be your model. His personality is infectious . . . people just like playing with him."

Bordick was described by many colleagues as an all-around, reliable player who could throw, hit, and play defense, and could always be expected to do his best and play hard. His former University of Maine coach, John Winkin, said, "He will do whatever it takes to help your team win." He spent seven years in Oakland as the team's main shortstop, hitting .300 in 1992.

In 1996, Bordick signed with the Baltimore Orioles, and was quickly assigned to take over as shortstop for the fabled "Iron Man," Cal Ripken Jr., when the team moved Ripken to third base.

Bordick proved a good choice. In 1997, the Orioles made it to postseason play, losing the American League Championship series to the Cleveland Indians. In 1998, he hit 13 home runs and led the league in sacrifice hits with 15.

His best season was 2000, when he was selected for his only All-Star Game. He had a career high of 20 home runs that year with 80 RBIs (runs batted in). His final batting total was .285 with 30 doubles.

That summer, the New York Mets lost their shortstop and traded four players to the Orioles to "borrow" Bordick for the rest of the season. In his first at bat for the Mets he hit a home run to tie up the game. A few days later, he drove in a run to win the game. The Mets were National League champions that year, In 56 games for the team, he batted .260 with 4 home runs, 8 doubles, 18 runs scored, and 21 RBIs. The Mets lost the World Series that year to the Yankees.

Bordick returned to Baltimore for two more seasons as a free agent. His best defensive season, and the best defensive season for a shortstop in major league history, was in 2002. He set a major league record for fielding percentages (a measure of the percentage of times a player properly handles a batted or thrown ball) with .998, fewest errors at 1, and the all-time record for consecutive errorless games at 110. He broke the record set by Rey Ordonez of the Mets, the shortstop he had replaced, when he reached 102 errorless games on September 21 playing against the Red Sox, a team that had tried vainly to acquire him from the Orioles. He had broken his predecessor Ripken's record earlier that month.

He finished his major league career in 2003 playing for the Toronto Blue Jays, batting .274 in 103 games. He went on to work as an instructor the Blue Jays, but returned to the Orioles in 2010 as minor league offensive coordinator, then bullpen coach. Since 2012 he has served as a broadcast color analyst for the Orioles on MASN. He and his wife and six children live in Maryland, but they have spent off-seasons in Maine.

In 1993, Bordick was inducted into the University of Maine Sports Hall of Fame and in 2005, the Maine Baseball Hall of Fame. In 2011, he was inducted into the Baltimore Orioles Hall of Fame. The field at Hampden Academy in named in his honor. And in his hometown of Winterport, the Winterport House of Pizza boasts a double cheeseburger named the Bordy Burger.

6

JOHN BOWER

Two-time Olympian and Nordic Ski Star

No doubt John Bower was destined to be a renowned skier. His first experience on skis was at age 14 months on a hill in his hometown of Auburn where he was born in 1940. It turned out well, since he went on to achieve several firsts in the sport.

He began competing at age nine and won his first blue ribbon for jumping at the Auburn Winter Carnival. When he was 10, he skied the challenging head wall at Tuckerman's Ravine on Mt. Washington in New Hampshire, New England's highest peak.

Bower competed all through his years at Edward Little High School, winning Alpine as well as Nordic events. He won Junior Nordic titles in cross-country and Nordic-combined in 1959, his junior year, skiing for the U.S. Eastern Amateur Ski Association.

He went on to Middlebury College in Vermont, where in 1961 he won the National Collegiate Athletic Association (NCAA) national championships in the Nordic combined—the school's first win in that event. The manager of the local ski hill, the Snow Bowl, called him "the best four-event skier we ever had." Bower earned the title "skimeister" for placing first in all four ski events at the hill every year. Like many great athletes, he was talented in more than one sport and played baseball for Middlebury as well.

Next step, Europe: He joined the Federation Internationale Ski (FIS) (or International Ski Federation, the governing body for international winter ski events) in 1962, and made the FIS team to compete in the World Ski Championships at Zakopane, Poland. Bower made the European circuit with the team, impressing the Europeans with finishes that were as good as more experienced American skiers had done. For instance, he took sixth place in Nordic combined at the prestigious Holmenkollen Skifestival events in Oslo, the best ever finish by an American and in his first attempt. Europeans took note. He also placed 11th in cross-country and 5th in jumping.

Bower won his first European event in the Nordic combined in Lappeenranta, Finland, in 1963. Then he took a second place in Kuovola, Finland. Back home, he won the National Nordic Combined Championships (NNCC) in Franconia, New Hampshire, then graduated from Middlebury and joined the Army for two years. He won the NNCC championship three more times in 1966, 1967, and 1968.

He also competed in the Nordic combined in the Winter Olympics in Innsbruck in 1964 while on temporary duty with the U.S. ski team, and finished 15th. He competed in the event at the Olympics again in Grenoble 1968, where he finished 13th. Both were the highest finishes by an American.

But in 1968, he really impressed the Europeans and everyone else by winning the King's Cup at the Holmenkollen in Oslo, the first non-Scandinavian ever to win the cup. The prize is awarded for best overall score which Bower achieved by winning the cross-country event and finishing fourth in ski jumping. This historic victory won him an audience with the king of Norway and a White House dinner invitation when the king visited Washington, D.C.

Referred to in news stories as "one of Maine's most accomplished and recognized sports figures," Bower was named to the U.S. Ski Hall of Fame in 1969. He was also inducted into the Maine Ski Hall of Fame in 2003, the year it was established. He joined the first class of the new Auburn-Lewiston Hall of Fame in 1984 and was in the first class of the Middlebury Athletics Hall of Fame in 2015.

After his illustrious career in competition, Bower launched another illustrious career in coaching. He returned to Middlebury College as Panther ski coach from 1969 to 1975, when he left to coach the United

States Ski Association Nordic Team. After that he did two stints as Nordic Director of the U.S. Ski Team from 1975 to 1980 and again from 1988 to 1992.

When he retired from coaching, he and his wife Bonnie moved to Park City, Utah, where he became the first director of the Utah Winter Sports Park, now the Utah Olympic Park, when it opened in 1989. Several 2002 Winter Olympic competitions were held there. Bower helped design the ski jumps for those Olympics. He also helped develop programs at the park from 1990 through 1999.

In 2015, the Bowers sold their Utah home, bought a motor home, and set off on new adventures, visiting the Canadian Rockies, Arizona, and doing volunteer work in St. Louis and at a Maine boys' camp. Bower died on June 6, 2017, at age 76.

"John Bower is a great example of a highly accomplished skier who dedicated his entire life to helping other athletes," said U.S. Ski & Snowboard President and CEO Tiger Shaw at the time of Bower's death. "In particular, his work in developing the Utah Olympic Park leading up to the 2002 Olympics was a key part of the legacy that is still positively impacting athletes today."

"His record was so impressive that he was like a god to his skiers, yet he cared about them as individuals. He's as fair a person as you'll ever see in your life," said Howard Kelton, long-time ski patrolman at Middlebury's ski hill, the Snow Bowl in Hancock, Vermont. "He never wanted to be in the limelight. No one ever said a bad word about John."

7

CHET BULGER

Offensive Tackle, NFL Champ, Teacher, and Coach

Chester Noyes "Chet" Bulger, born September 18, 1917, in Rumford, had the career distinction of being a top lineman on the last Cardinals team to win a National Football League (NFL) championship.

Chet attended St. Stephen's High School in Rumford, where he participated in football, basketball, and track. He captained the Falcons football team and in his senior year, took the team to a state championship. He was All-State tackle that year as well.

But that wasn't all. He was captain of the track team, set a state record in shot put, and won first place in discus, and led the field event to state championships in 1935 and 1936.

The doctor told him to take the rest of the season off when he broke some ribs as a sophomore playing against South Portland. Instead, his mother told him to put on his practice clothes and get out there. He continued to play despite the coach's objections.

The 6-foot, 3-inch Bulger was recruited by Auburn College in Auburn, Alabama, and attended on a track and field scholarship. He pretty quickly joined the football team where he was coached by Jack Meagher, a former Notre Dame great. At Auburn, he also set a Southeastern Conference discus record that lasted for many years.

Following graduation from Auburn, Bulger joined the Marines. After his 1942 discharge, the Chicago Cardinals Pro-Football team (later the St. Louis Cardinals) signed him. The Cardinals are the oldest continuously run professional football team in the United States, started as an amateur team in 1896 and joined the NFL as a charter member in 1920.

Bulger played for the team for seven years from 1942 to 1949, during the era of leather helmets, when Chicago had two pro football teams. Pro footballers didn't make much money then, and they often played to smaller crowds than high school teams. Bulger was an All-Pro tackle from 1943 through 1946. Then in 1947, the Cardinals won the World's Championship, besting the Philadelphia Eagles in Wrigley Field with the help of the team's All-Pro offensive line. Bulger was chosen All-Pro Lineman of the Year by the *Chicago Tribune*.

Even though the team was playing better in 1948, averaging 33 points a game, the Cardinals lost the championship to the Eagles in a 7-0 game played in a snowstorm. The Cards didn't play for the title again until the 2009 Super Bowl, which they lost to the Pittsburgh Steelers. Bulger left the Cardinals for the Detroit Lions for his last year of NFL play, and turned down offers from the Chicago Bears because he preferred the Cardinals. He retired from professional play for good in 1951.

He spent the next 31 years teaching and coaching track and the Meteor football team, winding up as athletic director at De La Salle Institute. Bulger was such a beloved faculty member at this private Catholic high school in Chicago that in 2007 the school named the main athletic field in his honor, and an event, The Chet Bulger Society's Blue-Gold Benefit. He retired in 1982, but stayed involved in the development program into the early 1990s.

While he never lived in Maine again, he stayed in touch with friends, kept up with the high school football program, and always spoke fondly of his childhood in Rumford.

"I'm so proud to have played for that high school," he told an interviewer. "To this day, I believe all of my success rested with the coaches I had there."

Bulger had five children with his wife, the former Harriet Cutter of Westbrook. He left Chicago to live in Virginia in retirement and died in Fairfax, Virginia, on February 18, 2009, at age 91.

Bulger received many other honors. His hometown of Rumford dedicated Chet Bulger Field to him at their athletic complex. In 1969, he was named on the All-Time, All-Cardinal team as defensive tackle. He was inducted into the Chicago Catholic League Coaches Association Hall of Fame in 2014 as an athlete and coach. He was inducted into the Maine Sports Hall of Fame in 1981, the De La Salle Institute Sports Hall of Fame, and the Chicagoland Sports Hall of Fame.

8

BILL "ROUGH" CARRIGAN

Red Sox Catcher, Manager, Coach of Babe Ruth

William Francis "Bill" Carrigan was born in Lewiston, October 22, 1883, youngest of three children born to Irish immigrant parents. His dad, John, was a storekeeper and deputy sheriff and his older brother, also John, was a talented pitcher. His brother pressed Bill into service to catch for him while he practiced.

Bill developed a taste for the game, played sandlot ball, and continued as a star player at Lewiston High school, where he also played football and a game called roller polo—a game like hockey on roller skates. Brother John convinced Bill to drop that game because he got into too many fights.

An injury curtailed John's baseball chances, but Bill went on to Holy Cross College in Worcester, Massachusetts, where he played ball for two years. During that time, his coach persuaded him to switch from infield to catcher. At the end of two years, Carrigan signed a major league contract with the Boston Americans, soon to become the Red Sox. Despite his athletic prowess, a football injury he sustained during his school years slowed him down in his major league career.

Baseball was different in this "Dead Ball Era," roughly from 1900 to 1919. Balls were not standard, were described as nearly soft, and the same ball was used throughout the game. Home runs were rare, so bunts, singles, and stolen bases were primary game-winning strategies.

The Mainer's debut in Boston came in 1906 when he quickly replaced the starting catcher. His first year, he was one of the Boston catchers to play against the Philadelphia Athletics in the American League's longest game, 24 innings. Ironically one of the opposing team pitchers was another Mainer, "Iron Man Jack" Coombs of Freeport.

Carrigan quickly earned the nickname "Rough" from the press, partly because of the way he dominated home, blocking a runner's path often by sitting on the plate, which caused a fair number of collisions and fights. This tendency also won him the nickname "The Human Stonewall."

"You might as well try to move a stone wall," Chicago White Sox manager Nixey Callahan once said of Carrigan. Off the field Carrigan was known as well-spoken and intelligent. On the field, the 5-foot, 9-inch, 175-pounder was known as one of the game's best fighters.

Around 1910, the team was experiencing a lot of interpersonal difficulties, with factions including coaches and players split along Protestant and Catholic lines. Some players, held strong anti-Catholic sentiments and supported their manager, Jake Stahl, who shared their views. Catholics like Carrigan sided with the team's co-owner, Jimmy McAleer. Finally, in midseason 1913, McAleer fired Stahl, making Carrigan a player-manager. Some accounts say a fistfight Carrigan won against a Protestant teammate helped establish his authority.

That year, Boston moved up to finish in fourth place. That same year, Carrigan convinced the Red Sox to buy the contract of a young Baltimore player, George Herman "Babe" Ruth. In 1914, Carrigan led the Sox to second place. The following year and the year after that, he brought them back-to-back wins in the World Series. It was the first and last time the Sox would win back-to-back series for nearly a hundred years, until 2007.

The first series, in 1915, the Sox played against the Phillies and won four straight games. The series also marked the first time a president, Woodrow Wilson, attended a World Series game. In 1916, the Sox played the Brooklyn Dodgers (then known as the Robins) and won in 4–1. Carrigan put himself in as catcher in game four. Besides his legendary back-to-back series wins, Carrigan also caught three no-hitters in his career.

He and the young Babe Ruth became friends. Ruth was a party animal, so Carrigan's method of controlling the left-handed pitcher's wild behavior was to make Ruth his roommate during the season.

Once Ruth was arrested and Carrigan refused to bail him out until the next morning, saying at least "I'll know where he is tonight." In those championship years, Babe Ruth's records were 18–8 and 23–12. Ruth credited Carrigan as the best coach he ever had.

"Nobody could have made Ruth the great pitcher and the great hitter he was but himself. . . . But, breaking in, he had to be disciplined to save him from probably becoming his own worst enemy," wrote Carrigan in the *Boston Daily Record* newspaper. "And I saw to it that he was disciplined."

Just before the 1915 season, Carrigan received a papal dispensation and married Beulah Bartlett, a Protestant woman and a lifelong friend. During the successful 1916 season, Carrigan informed the team he wanted to retire to spend more time with his wife and new daughter. Later the couple had two more children.

After Carrigan left, Ruth was sold to the Yankees in 1919, despite a stellar season in which he broke the single-season MLB home run record, following two other years when he won 23 games as a pitcher, and despite playing on three Red Sox World Series teams. Thus began the 86-year "Curse of the Bambino" when the Red Sox could not win a series.

Carrigan returned to Lewiston to partner in a group that owned around 50 vaudeville and movie theaters. By 1922, he sold his interest in the group.

The Red Sox enticed him back as manager starting in 1927. When the team finished last for three seasons, he resigned again at the end of 1929. After baseball, he went into banking and in 1953, was named president of People's Savings Bank in Lewiston. His wife died in 1958, and Bill died July 8, 1969, at Central Maine Hospital in Lewiston at age 85. In 1946, he was elected to the Honor Roll of Baseball in Cooperstown, New York, at that time the only honor the national Hall of Fame bestowed on managers. He was named to the Holy Cross Hall of Fame in 1968, the Maine Baseball Hall of Fame in 1969, in 1976 the Maine Sports Hall of Fame, and in 2004, he was inducted into the Boston Red Sox Hall of Fame.

9

WALTER CASE JR.

Maine's Premier and Controversial Harness Racer

Harness racers are not the best-known or best-compensated athletes in the United States, but the drivers apparently don't care. It appears to be an obsessive sport, with drivers competing in many races a day to make a living, sometimes six days a week, especially on smaller, regional tracks where the purses are low.

Walter Case Jr., "Casey," is a good example. Case has been described by fans as one of the greatest harness racers the United States has produced. Whether that's true or not, he has been the holder of several records. He once set a record with 10 wins on one program in one day in 1999. Case won several titles at Yonkers Raceway and Northfield Park.

He was born into harness racing in 1961, and grew up in a trailer behind the old Lewiston Raceway. Case's father, Walter Sr., was heavily involved in harness racing, his brother (now deceased) was a promising trainer, and his sister Kelly is a winning racer. Case reportedly was obsessed from the first time he drove, and dropped out of school to get his racing license at 16. Observers said when he won his first race, there was no stopping him.

At the top of his career in the late 1990s when he was earning $5,000 a week, Case said he would hire a limo on Saturday nights for $1,000 to drive him home to Lisbon Falls from whichever New York track he raced at that night. However, when his career was at its peak he also racked up many violations. In 1999 he had 150 days suspensions, 40 racing violations, and $6,000 in fines, causing New York and New Jersey to refuse him a license.

Again in 2003, Case lost his license to race following 178 days' worth of suspensions, mostly in New York and mostly for failing to keep his feet in the sulky stirrups, but also for drunk driving or failing drug tests. Out of work, he ate too much, drank too much, took a lot of pills, and saw his weight balloon from 140 to 185 pounds. During this period, he attacked his estranged wife with a knife, was convicted of a felony, sentenced to five years in an Ohio jail, and served four as a model prisoner.

After being released from jail in 2008, he had no license for several years, and Case admitted he had been high on drugs or alcohol during nearly all of his career. The one year he was not high was his best. In 1998, he set the record for most driving wins in the country in one year with 1,077, a record that lasted for seven years. In 1991, 1992, and 1998, he was voted Harness Tracks of America Driver of the Year. With 11,049 wins, in 2017 he was still ranked the eighth winningest racer in the country. Usually driving six days a week during much of his career, he averaged three wins a day for one year. In 1992, Case posted 843 wins, then a world record. Maine racing fans believe he could have been the world's best without the drinking and drugs.

While his career didn't end after his felony conviction, Case failed to retrieve his license to race anywhere for nine years, until 2017 when he was allowed to race conditionally in Maine. He returned to Scarborough Downs and won three races in his first appearance. When the announcer was introducing competitions in the first race, a long, loud ovation from the crowd at the mention of Case's name interrupted the announcement. A throng of well-wishers crowded him in the winners' circle when he took first place in the second race. He has not resumed his career, but is still the second-winningest harness racer in Maine.

10

KIRSTEN CLARK-RICKENBACH

One of Maine's Fastest Skiers

Alpine skier Kirsten Clark was born in Richmond, April 23, 1977. Like many successful skiers from Maine, she started skiing at three, competing at seven, and honed her craft at Sugarloaf Mountain in Carrabassett Valley.

She attended Carrabassett Valley Academy, a private high school with a focus on skiing and snowboarding, graduating in 1995. While still in school, she became Junior Olympics downhill champion in 1994, and earned a bronze medal in Super G at the competition held at Sugarloaf.

Downhill and Super G were her primary events, although in 1997, Clark won the North American giant slalom championship. After that, she began focusing more on speed events. She raced in three Junior World Championships.

Nicknamed "Clarkie" by her teammates, the 5-foot, 4-inch Clark began competing in the World Cup in a giant slalom event in January of 1997, the same year she first competed in the World Championships. In December of that year, she competed in the World Cup Super G, qualifying for the 1998 Winter Olympics in Nagano, where she raced in the downhill, the combination, and the Super-G.

In 1998, she won the downhill in the U.S. Championships, beginning a four-year consecutive streak that no one has beaten since. She won the U.S. title again in 2006. All in all, she earned 12 U.S. Championship medals, seven U.S. titles and 201 World Cup starts, reached the podium in eight World Cup contests including one first, in her 13-year career on the U.S. Ski Team.

Clark had 28 top ten finishes in World Cup events, but in February of 2001, she came in first in the World Cup downhill event. Clark also competed in the 2002 World Cup, coming in third in the Super-G in St. Moritz. She competed in the 2002 Winter Olympics in Salt Lake City. In 2003, Clark took silver in the Super G at the World Championships in St. Moritz.

She suffered ligament tears in both knees and fractured her wrist in a downhill race accident, when she hit the safety netting headfirst at 60 mph during the 2004 World Cup in Haus, Austria. Forced to drop out of competition for six months, she raced again in the 2005 World Cup despite an infection that developed as a result of a follow-up procedure on her knee. That year she won the U.S. Alpine Championship women's downhill held at Sugarloaf.

She competed again in the 2006 Winter Olympics in Turin, Italy, suffered another crash during the World Cup that year, and retired from competition in 2007.

Clark married Andreas Rickenbach, a former World Cup racer and coach. They have two daughters, and together run Rickenbach Development & Construction in the Squaw Valley, California, area where they live, and where she coaches skiing on weekends.

Her parents live in Richmond. Her older brother, Sean, is a former Bates College ski champion and Jackson Hole ski coach. Kirsten says she began skiing just to chase Sean down the hill at Sugarloaf.

Besides being a dedicated, passionate athlete, Clark is respected by coaches and teammates for her leadership qualities, willingness to help young athletes, and for just being an all-around good person.

Fellow retired U.S. Ski Team and Olympian Lindsey Vonn said of her, "Clarkie was always someone I looked up to."

Clark was inducted into the Maine Sports Hall of Fame in 2001 and the Maine Ski Hall of Fame in 2010. In 2012, she was inducted into the U.S. Ski and Snowboard Hall of Fame.

"COLBY JACK" COOMBS

American League Record Holder

John Wesley "Jack" or "Colby Jack" Coombs was born in the small farming community of LeGrand, Iowa, on November 18, 1882. Four years later, his family moved to another farm, near Kennebunk.

Coombs was an all-around athlete all through high school and college. He played baseball at Freeport High School and then at Coburn Classical Prep School in Waterville.

At Colby, the 6-foot, 185-lb Coombs also played football and tennis, and ran track. He captained his baseball and basketball teams, was known as a particularly speedy runner in football, and proved to be New England's fastest sprinter of his time. He could run the 100-yard dash in 10.2 seconds.

But he really excelled at baseball, playing every position when necessary. He led his Colby team to several college championships and spent summers playing semi-pro baseball throughout New England.

No academic slouch, Coombs majored in chemistry and joined Delta Upsilon fraternity. He planned to make a career of chemistry and intended to head to graduate work at the Massachusetts Institute of Technology. Instead, he was signed for the majors during his senior year, and joined the Philadelphia Athletics three weeks after graduation from Colby.

He wasted no time establishing himself in the majors. His first game in the "Deadball Era" with the Athletics, Coombs pitched a 7-hit shutout, beating the Washington Senators 3–1. It was a banner year for Coombs and his team. The newcomer pitched an entire 24-inning game against Boston, the longest game in the American League and a pitching record that still stands. Philly won 3–2. Coombs ended the season with a 10–10 record and a 2.50 ERA.

The next few years weren't terrible, although not as good as the first; however, Coombs and the team bounced back in 1910. He won three games in the World Series where the Athletics beat the Chicago Cubs, pitching the entire three games within six days. He also had five hits in the series in 13 at-bats, for a series total of .385.

That year, Coombs was responsible for one of the best pitching seasons in professional baseball history, earning a record of 31–9 aided by his fastball and drop curve ball. He led the league with 31 wins, 45 games played, and an American League record of 13 shutouts that still stands. He also set a few other records, later to be broken, such as 53 consecutive scoreless innings in September.

During that record-setting season when he earned the nickname "Iron Man," he also pitched a total of 353 innings, in 11 of which he held the opposing team to one run. Coombs finished 35 of the games he started and won 18 out of 19 starts in July alone. It was a banner year in other ways as well, Coombs also married Mary, a woman from Palestine, Texas—a town where the couple maintained a winter home for the rest of their lives.

In 1911, the Athletics again won the pennant, faced the New York Giants in the World Series, and defeated them 4–2. Coombs won a spectacular game 3 in extra innings, allowing only three hits, but he pulled his groin badly in game 5, forced to leave the game in the tenth inning. He was still affected by the injury in 1912, and although he missed a month of play, he still won 21 games and lost only 10.

The next year, Coombs ended up hospitalized with typhoid fever in his spine. He spent 17 weeks in bed with weights to strengthen his spine and hardly played in 1914. In 1915, after missing most of two seasons, being released and signing with the Brooklyn Robins/Dodgers, Coombs bounced back briefly. He won 15 and lost 10. In 1916, he won one World Series game for Brooklyn, although the team lost the series to the Red Sox. His performances in 1917 and 1918 suffered, although he pitched his 35th and last shutout against the Cincinnati Reds in 1918, and retired in August of that year. In his career, he never lost a World Series game. He played in five and won five.

After that, he managed the Phillies for 62 games with little success and played one last year in 1920, ending his 14-year career with a .235 batting average, 123 runs, 4 home runs, and 100 RBI.

He found his next passion as a college baseball coach, starting at Williams for three years, then Princeton for three more, and finally, at Duke for 24 years. His record with the Duke Blue Devils was 382–171, including seven college and five Southern Conference championships, and 21 players who went to the majors. Duke players described "Mr. College Baseball" as "beloved," funny, charming, direct, and friendly.

When he reached Duke's mandatory retirement age of 70, he retired to Palestine in 1952 where he ran annual high school baseball clinics. He died at home of a heart attack in 1957.

Coombs wrote an instructional book in 1938, *Baseball—Individual Play and Team Strategy*, that was used by college and high school baseball teams around the country. According to Maine's beloved writer John Gould, who also attended Freeport High, Coombs returned for years to play an inning in an Old Timers' game against the high school team, and coached a team in Maine's Pine Tree League.

Both Colby College and Duke University named their baseball fields for him. He has been inducted into the Des Moines Register's Iowa Sports Hall of Fame, the Duke University Athletics Hall of Fame in 1977, the North Carolina Sports Hall of Fame, the Collegiate Baseball Coaches Hall of Fame, the Maine Baseball Hall of Fame in 1969, the Maine Sports Hall of Fame in 1977, and the Phillies Wall of Famers in 1992. He was a charter inductee into the now-defunct Collegiate Baseball Coaches Hall of Fame. The only Hall of Fame that has eluded him is the national Baseball Hall of Fame, although many believe he has been unfairly omitted.

12

CORNELIA "FLY ROD" CROSBY

Maine's First Official Guide, Fly Fisher, and
Marketer of the Outdoors

Cornelia Thurza Crosby, the woman who would put Maine's wilderness on the map for outdoor recreation such as hunting and fishing, was an unlikely candidate for the job.

Born November 10, 1854, in Phillips, Maine, a town just south of the Rangeley Lakes region, Cornelia's family was severely affected by tuberculosis: Her father died of it when she was small and the disease caused her to be sickly throughout her life.

She inherited $600 in her teens and used it to pay tuition for St. Catherine's Hall, an Episcopal school for girls in Augusta. After graduating, she worked as a bank teller, but recurring sick spells that sometimes left her bedridden forced her to take a lot of time off to recuperate.

A doctor once told her she would die without "abundant doses of fresh air." During one of her spells, around 1878 when she was 24 years old, she was expected to die. She was taken to the foot of Mount Blue where she went fishing and caught her first "speckled beauty" as she called Maine's trout.

In a day when women rarely achieved fame, especially for pursuits considered to be strictly the province of men, Cornelia not only rose above her physical weakness, but became a fly-fishing legend. A Farmington fishing rod maker, Charles E. Wheeler, presented her with a 5-oz. bamboo rod and the rest is history.

She reportedly caught 200 fish in one day, and some say she caught 2,500 trout during the summer of 1893. She became a regular fixture at Rangeley during fishing season and her reputation as an angler spread. By 1886 she had earned the nickname "Fly Rod."

Crosby had taken a job at a telegraph office, but returning to work after one of her sickly bouts, she discovered she was an early victim of technology. In August of 1882, the telephone had rendered her job obsolete, so she began writing a column, Fly Rod's Notebook, for a local paper, mostly about her own adventures.

The column's popularity spread, leading to syndication around the country. The information she included about Maine's sporting camps interested travelers. The Maine Central Railroad spotted a marketing opportunity and hired her to promote the wilderness industry directly, knowing travelers would need the rails to get to the place she dubbed "Maine—the Nation's Playground." Her biographers subtitled their book about her, *The Woman Who Marketed Maine*.

At the First Annual Sportsmen's Exposition in New York's Madison Square Garden in 1895, she organized Maine's exhibit. The following year, she shocked attendees by appearing in a green leather hunting outfit sporting a scandalous mid-calf length skirt. She completed the outfit with a tailored jacket, a red sweater, a peaked red and green hat, and a pair of green lace-up boots. Crowds thronged to watch her fly-fishing demonstrations and stayed to hear her describe the wonders of Maine's great outdoors.

Her displays at the expositions included a log cabin, examples of taxidermy, and fish tanks with live Maine salmon and trout. She met Annie Oakley at the 1896 show and they became fast friends. For roughly a decade, she attended the New York shows and similar shows in Boston and Philadelphia. At the Boston Food Fair in 1897, her mother, Thurza Cottle Porter Crosby, gave spinning demonstrations at the event, and others made Penobscot baskets.

The Maine Fish and Game Association hired her to lobby the Maine Legislature to register the state's hunting and fishing guides. During the Sportsmen's Exposition in 1897, she received word a bill had passed requiring a license for guides and some funds to protect fish and game in Maine.

In 1898, she was awarded license number 1, making her the first official Registered Maine Guide. She served as a model of independence and athleticism for young women and was renowned, honored, and enjoyed the status of a legend for many years of her life, but she was modest, once describing herself this way: "I am a plain woman of uncertain age, standing six feet in my stockings . . . . I scribble a bit for various sporting journals, and I would rather fish any day than go to heaven."

Despite her sickliness, she lived to be 92, and died the day after her birthday. The Fly Rod Crosby Trail, honoring the western Maine hero, starts in Phillips and continues 45 miles through the communities of the High Peaks Region. Built and maintained by volunteers, the trail aims to show visitors the region as seen through Crosby's writings with sections for hiking, biking, ATV riding, and kayaking.

13

JOEY GAMACHE

Maine's Only World Boxing Title Winner

Joey Gamache was born in Lewiston on May 20, 1966, a scrappy boxer from a fighting town that spawned many pugilists. Lewiston attracted world attention as the site of the short-lived Sonny Liston—Muhammad Ali world heavyweight fight of May 25, 1965, at the Central Maine Youth Center. Ali was defending his title when he decked Liston one minute into the first round.

Long before that fight, boxing had been a wildly popular sport in the city, boasting many talented contenders and huge audiences, but prior to cable TV and social media, the fighters had a tough time gaining recognition outside Maine. By 1974, Maine had stopped issuing rankings for boxers because there were so few.

Gamache might have missed boxing altogether. At age 10, he was playing third base in Little League when his dad suggested that working out at the gym might strengthen his pitching arm. He fell in love with the gym and that was the end of baseball. It also didn't hurt that Joey watched Sugar Ray Leonard on TV in the Montreal Summer Olympics that same year, 1976. Helping revive interest in boxing also in 1976 was the runaway success of Sylvester Stallone's movie *Rocky*.

A legend in Lewiston, Gamache is the only Maine fighter ever to win a world boxing title. Before he turned pro, he won three New England Golden Gloves titles and a bronze medal at the 1984 Olympic trials.

He credits his father Joe Gamache Sr., legendary Lewiston trainers Tony Lampron, Teddy Atlas, and Roland Fortin, as well as promoter Johnny Bos for his boxing success.

"Fighters are driven by destitution. They see boxing as an opportunity for the family to improve their lifestyle. It was a whole team, and I couldn't have done it if any of those people weren't involved," Gamache once said. "And the same goes for the fans. They supported me from day one."

He turned professional in 1987 and won his first 28 fights including a few in France, capturing the World Boxing Association (WBA) super featherweight title when he knocked out Jerry Ngobeni in the 10th round at the Lewiston Raceway in 1991. The next year, he beat Chil-Sung Chun for the WBA lightweight title. He lost the lightweight title to Tony Lopez in an 11th round TKO, and failed to regain it in 1994 when he challenged then-champion Orzubek Nazarov.

A few violent knockouts by fighters Nazarov and Julio Cesar Chavez seriously curtailed his fighting, but a brutal second round knockout by Arturo Gatti in 2000 landed Gamache in the hospital with a brain injury, ending his career. Gamache sued the New York State Athletic Commission claiming Gatti weighed significantly more than the contracted weight at the time of the fight. Although the judge did not rule the injury was caused by the weight difference, he did find the state negligent at the weigh-in, so Gamache considered the decision a victory. His was not the only claim against the Commission around that time.

Gamache retired with a 55–4 record and 36 KOs, then turned to promoting fights in Lewiston, trained high-level boxers in Europe for five years, and ended up training fighters in New York. In early 2019, he was blindsided by an attacker on a New York City street, requiring hospitalization for a badly broken jaw.

When he returns to Maine he sometimes helps Joe Sr. train fighters at his Gamache Boxing Club in Lewiston.

(14)

ANNA GOODALE

Olympic Medalist and Hall-of-Fame Rower

Anna P. Goodale did not discover the passion that won her an Olympic medal until she reached college. While attending Syracuse University and majoring in illustration, the Maine native tried competitive rowing and discovered she had quite a knack for it.

In 2003 and 2005, the 6-footer was a first-team Division 1 All-American at Syracuse and in 2004, a second-team Division 1 All-American. Before her graduation from Syracuse in 2005, she was also named a National Scholar-Athlete, a Big East Academic All-Star, and twice a first-team Mid-Atlantic Region All-Star. As a senior, Goodale received Syracuse's most prestigious student athlete award, the Soladay Award from the Syracuse athletics department

Born in Montville on March 18, 1983, Goodale grew up on a sheep farm, spending most of her time outdoors, and was home-schooled until she was nine.

She attended Camden Hills Regional High School, where she competed in soccer, basketball, and on the All-State Academic Team, and won entry into the National Honor Society.

As a child, she said the Olympics were one of her favorite things to watch on television because she admired the athletes who worked hard to reach that level. She didn't expect she would be one of them someday.

After college, she joined the U.S. Rowing team, competing nationally and internationally. Her crew won gold in the Women's Eight at the 2008 Olympic Games in Beijing where one of her crewmates was fellow Mainer, Ellie Logan of Boothbay Harbor. Their team won the 2,000-meter final with a time of 6 minutes, 5.34 seconds, two seconds ahead of the second-place Netherlands.

In other international competition, Goodale also won four World Championships and three gold medals at the Head of the Charles Regatta between 2006 and 2010. On the national level, she also took four first place finishes and several other top awards.

She officially retired from competitive rowing in 2011 to pursue a career in illustration and travel with family members. When she retired, Goodale was ranked as the sixth most decorated rower by World Rowing.

Goodale moved to Spokane, Washington, at the same time that Gonzaga University was looking for an assistant rowing coach for their Bull Dogs team. She surprised herself by accepting the job and helped them win a West Coast Conference competition and end their 2015 season in 17th place at the NCAA Championships, the best in the school's history.

"I never thought I would be interested in coaching (or any good at it for that matter)," Goodale said. "A lot of parts of coaching are out of my comfort zone and it's been a huge growth opportunity for me."

After a year at Gonzaga, she accepted a job coaching the women's team at Ohio State University, where she remained as head novice coach for the Women's Rowing Team for four years.

In 2011, she was inducted into the Midcoast (Maine) Sports Hall of Fame. In 2014, she was inducted, along with the rest of her Olympic team, into the National Rowing Hall of Fame. In 2015, she was inducted into the Maine Sports Hall of Fame.

In 2019, she returned to her hometown. Goodale was hired as first executive director and head coach of Megunticook Rowing in Camden, a nonprofit community rowing program for Midcoast Maine. She lives in Camden with her husband and two sons.

Among her many talents, Goodale is also a freelance illustrator who has always planned to illustrate children's books. Her great-great grandfather was All-American football captain Tom Shevlin and her gray-great-great grandfather, Paul Mortonk, served as Theodore Roosevelt's

Secretary of the Navy. Her other interests include hiking, cross-country skiing, dog-sledding, camping, kayaking, and traveling.

"I attribute a lot of my work ethic and character to growing up in Maine, being outside and taking full advantage of the wonderful sur- roundings that Maine has to offer. I've always loved being outside. When we hiked, I'd always be at the top of the mountain and then wait for everyone else to come," she said at her induction into the Maine Sports Hall of Fame.

"Having the opportunity to be outside and practice that determina- tion is something I'd always look forward to. Here in Maine we have a great opportunity for people being athletic, because we are surrounded by the natural world."

15

BERND HEINRICH

Ultramarathon Record-Setter and Naturalist Extraordinaire

Bernd Heinrich has had the kind of interesting life that might have destroyed another person. Instead, Heinrich turned adversity into self-reliance and overachievement to become an ultramarathon record-holder and a renowned scientist.

Heinrich was born April 19, 1940, in Germany. His parents were biologists who left right after World War II, just before their home became East Germany. The family—Bernd, his sister, and parents—subsisted in a forest near the Elbe River until they could emigrate to the United States in 1951, settling in Wilton, Maine. With few opportunities to earn money, his father collected birds to sell as museum specimens.

Bernd was practically born a naturalist. Between growing up in the woods of Germany, Poland, and Maine, and learning about the creatures of nature from his insect taxonomist father, Heinrich also began running in the woods for the joy and exercise. He credited his father with teaching him to be still and unflappable, traits he used as discipline in long-distance running.

When his parents were offered an opportunity to collect specimens in Mexico and Africa, Heinrich and his sister were sent to the Good Will boarding school in Hinckley for disadvantaged and homeless children. Heinrich recalled those years as unhappy, but he escaped to the woods when possible, eventually clearing a half-mile stretch through the woods for running.

As a high school junior, he joined the cross-country team, winning nine meets in a row and setting course records. The University of Maine coach, Ed Styyma, had heard about him and Heinrich believes Styma helped get him into the university and assured his financial aid. Freshman year injuries limited his competition, but during the next three years, he ran cross-country, indoor, and outdoor track.

"I owe a lot to running," Heinrich once said. "It's probably the only reason I went to college." He called running "simple and direct" because it could be practiced without fancy equipment, at any time in any place.

The Bears placed second in the Yankee Conference in cross-country in 1961, and seventh in New England—the best team east of the Mississippi. The next year, they were second again and fifth in New England. But in 1963, the Bears finished first in the Yankee Conference and second in New England.

Their record in indoor track was even more impressive. They lost only two meets between 1961 and 1964. In outdoor track, the University of Maine won the Yankee Conference every year from 1961 to 1965. However, Heinrich missed a chance to shine when he took a year off to work on a zoological expedition in Africa with his parents. When he returned in 1963, a series of mishaps kept him from setting records.

Heinrich earned his bachelor's and master's from the University of Maine in biology, finished in 1966, and went to UCLA for a PhD in zoology. He pretty much gave up racing to become a world expert on bees. He continued to run on his own, often on the UCLA track, but rarely competed. While teaching at University of California at Berkeley, he became interested in marathons, and in 1975, signed up for the Boston Marathon. A knee pain sent him to an orthopedic surgeon who advised him against running. However, he ran and finished in 46th place with a time of. 2:23.

In 1979, he signed up for the Golden Gate Marathon. Although strong winds blew on this hot day, Heinrich kept a steady pace to find himself in third place a mile before the end. He maintained his steady pace while the leaders continued to slow down, and he won with a time of 2:29. Since he was 39, it was his last year to compete as a regular runner.

Missing the forest of the east, Heinrich relocated to teach at the University of Vermont in 1980 but also bought a tract of wooded land in

Maine, near where he grew up. He also entered the Boston Marathon, winning in the master's division in 2:25:25, a full two minutes ahead of the second-place runner. The same year, he ran the west Valley Marathon in California. He placed third with 2:22:34, his personal best, but missed qualifying for the Olympic trials by 40 seconds.

Next came ultramarathoning. He realized his stamina allowed him to pass other marathoners near the end of races, so he decided to try running further. The Road Runners Club of America offered a championship combined 50 mile and 100-K race. In October of 1981, not long after surgery for a torn meniscus and despite strong headwinds, Heinrich passed the 50-mile mark just 15 minutes under the world masters record, at 5:10:12. He kept running and finished the 100 K at 6:38:20, setting a new world masters record in his first ultramarathon and beating the old record by 43 minutes. His record stood for 15 years.

Heinrich's drug of choice for getting through races is cranberry juice. He drank 1.5 gallons during a Chicago race.

The following year, he tackled a 50-mile race in Brunswick—the Rowdy 50 Miler, where he won by 37 minutes over 36 runners. In 1983, he entered the Rowdy Ultimate 24-hour race and set another record, running 156 miles and 1,388 yards, often in 90-degree heat. He spent a week in intensive care when he collapsed at the finish line, but during that race, he set another American record for the 200 K at 18:30:10. The next year in Ottawa he beat the record for 100 miles by an hour and set another U.S. record by covering 95 miles in 12 hours on the track. All these were open records, not masters records, even though Heinrich was in his 40s.

But running is his avocation. Heinrich's profession is physiological ecologist and entomologist. He is considered the world's leading authority on the physiology of bumblebees and the sociology of ravens, although he is expert in other biological areas as well. He has written more than 20 books on a range of topics in the natural world, including *Ravens in Winter*, *The Snoring Bird*, *Bumblebee Economics*, and *Why We Run*. He has authored numerous scientific papers, and more than 100 articles in scientific journals.

He was named *Ultrarunner of the Year* three of the first four years of *Ultrarunning Magazine*. He was inducted into the Maine Sports Hall of Fame in 2000, the American Ultrarunning Association's Hall of Fame in

2008, and the Maine Running Hall of Fame in 1996—at that time only the second inductee to have held a world record. The other was Joan Benoit. In 2014, he was chosen for the University of Maine Alumni Association's Alumni Career Award for a lifetime of outstanding achievement and dedication.

16

JOHN ROLAND "BIG JOHN" HUARD

First University of Maine Player Elected to the
College Football Hall of Fame

John Huard was born in Waterville, March 9, 1944, and graduated from
Kents Hill School before going on to an illustrious college football career at the University of Maine in Orono from 1963 to 1966.

"Big John" Huard was a 6-foot, 220-pound linebacker when he led
University of Maine's Black Bears to the team's only bowl appearance—
the 1965 Tangerine Bowl in Orlando, Florida. He was twice named a
first team All-American for the university in 1965 and 1966. He was
also a two-time First-Team All-Yankee Conference player who had 22
tackles in his first game in 1964.

After graduation, he was signed by the Denver Broncos in the 1967
NFL football draft. He started every game of the first three seasons as
a middle linebacker with the Broncos, but suffered a knee injury at the
start of his fourth season. During his three seasons, he intercepted six
passes. He went on to the New Orleans Saints in 1971 but tore his Achil-
les tendon in the first game, ending his NFL career.

He recovered to play three seasons in the Canadian Football League
starting in 1973—one year with the Montreal Alouettes and two more
with the Toronto Argonauts.

When his career on the field ended, Huard began coaching, starting as an assistant, then rising to head coach with his alma mater, the

University of Maine. He moved on to Wolfville, Nova Scotia, to coach the Acadia University's Axemen team and won two Vanier Cups—the Canadian college football national championships—in 1979 and 1981.

Huard then moved to the short-lived United States Football League where he served as special teams coach of the Chicago Blitz. In 1987, he returned to Maine as head coach for the Maine Maritime Academy's Mariners football team until 1994. His last season, he led the Mariners to a championship in the New England Football Conference. During his seven-year tenure, he was twice named the New England Football Conference Coach of the Year.

After that, he went to coach at his other Maine alma mater—Kents Hill School. He wrapped up his coaching career in 2000 after a brief stint with the Argonauts.

Called "one of the greatest football players in state history," Huard has been honored by his town, his university, the state, and the national college hall of fame.

In 1986, he was the first football player inducted into the University of Maine Sports Hall of Fame. In 2003, he was the first player to be inducted into the Ring of Honor at Alfond Stadium in Orono. In 2014, Huard was the first Black Bear to be inducted into the College Football Hall of Fame.

In 2017, members of the 1965 Black Bear Tangerine Bowl team showed up in Waterville to celebrate Huard when he was honored by the town with his own monument at its Purnell Wrigley Field. The dedication took place on July 28, opening day of the New England Cal Ripken Baseball Championships. His monument was placed between those of John Winkin, a College Baseball Hall of Fame inductee, and Clyde Sukeforth, the Maine baseball scout who signed Jackie Robinson to his first major league baseball contract.

Huard is founder and president of the Northeast Turf/Eastern Builders that provides artificial turf for athletic fields. His company has donated turf to Acadia's Raymond Field at the University of Maine's Mahaney Dome. He's active with the Maine chapter of the National Football Foundation, volunteers with the Waterville Boys and Girls Club, and the Susan Curtis Foundation.

"John Huard is certainly one of our hometown heroes. His strong character, spirit, and love of the game started here in Waterville," said Alfond Youth Center CEO, Ken Walsh. "His legacy will remain strong within our community forever."

17

BARBARA KRAUSE

Basketball Legend

Some people are just overachievers and Freeport's own Barbara Krause is one who excelled on the basketball court and in academics.

Krause excelled at both sports and academics, even in middle school, led Freeport High School to state titles in basketball, field hockey, and softball. In 1976, her senior year, she led the team to a Class C State Championship, calling it "one of the most exciting, most special, most formative events of my life."

Basketball was definitely her calling. She went on to Bowdoin College in Brunswick, joined the basketball team, and averaged 22.3 points per game and had 14.9 rebounds during her one year there. Both still stand as records for Bowdoin in a single season. While there, she tried outdoor track for the first time, throwing discus, shot put, and javelin.

"Bowdoin College gave me an amazing freshman year, both academically and athletically," Krause said.

She then transferred to Duke University in North Carolina where she became a star of the basketball team, serving as team captain for two years, 1980 and 1981. In 1979, she set the single-game record in (Atlantic Coast Conference) ACC-only competitions with 23 rebounds against Georgia Tech. The statistic still holds as Duke's second-place record.

During the 1978–1979 season, she averaged 10.7 rebounds per game, leading the ACC for the year, and putting her third in the single-season records for Duke. In 1980, she attempted 17 free throws against Colorado, earning eighth-place ranking in Duke's single-game records.

Clearly, she's good at rebounds. Krause's 9.9 game average for three years is a tie for seventh best in ACC history and a Duke second-best record. She collected 732 rebounds in those three years, putting her tenth in Duke records.

The 5-foot, 10-inch Krause played power forward for the Blue Devils at Duke "against opponents who were almost always much taller than I." She was named All-State and also invited to try out for the Pan American Games in 1979.

In her era, women's sports were not included in the National Collegiate Athletic Association so they competed in the Association of Intercollegiate Athletics for Women, which meant they played all North Carolina schools. Title IX, the federal law passed in 1972 that extended equal access to sports for women, was just coming into its own.

Meanwhile, Krause was also busy excelling at academics. She graduated summa cum laude from Duke in 1981 with a double major in philosophy and German. She earned honors in German and was elected to Phi Beta Kappa.

Upon graduation, Krause headed for Germany for two years to play professional basketball with the country's best league, the Basketball Bundesliga League (BBL), before returning to the United States and law school.

"Having the opportunity to live in a different country, to become fluent in a different language, and to travel on my own and see some of the world—those experiences gave me perspectives that I value to this day," she said.

At Cornell Law School, she served as editor-in-chief of the *Cornell International Law Journal*, and graduated in 2000 with her JD degree in 1986.

Krause returned to Maine to serve as clerk for Judge Edward T. Gignoux in the Federal District Court, then became an associate and partner in a Portland law firm, representing towns and schools.

She went on to Cornell, where she served as a judicial administrator, an assistant secretary of the corporation, associate university council, and senior advisor to the president. From there, she moved to Skidmore College in 2006 to become executive director of the Office of the President. She went on to serve as deputy general counsel at Appalachian State University.

In 2009 Krause was honored by the Atlantic Coast Conference as an ACC legend for the basketball records she set and still holds. In 1999, she was inducted into the Maine Sports Hall of Fame, and in 2009, the New England Basketball Hall of Fame. In 2018, she was inducted into the Maine Basketball Hall of Fame.

"Basketball taught me so much about competing well—against myself, to be the best I could be; and against opponents, to be the best our team could be. It allowed me to explore what sort of a leader I could be."

18

RAY LEBEL

Maine Amateur Golf Legend

Raymond Lucien "Ray" Lebel, born April 22, 1923, in Lewiston, developed his passion for golf when he was only 10, and won his first club championship at the Martindale Country Club in Auburn at 14 where he was a caddy.

In 1940, he graduated from Lewiston High School, went on to Bliss Business College and worked at a bank for a year before joining the Navy to fight in World War II. As in his other areas of endeavor, Lebel excelled in the Navy. He became a fighter pilot, flew Hell Cats, attained the rank of ensign, earned two Distinguished Navy Crosses and five Air Medals.

Just before he joined the Navy in 1942, Lebel won the Maine Amateur championship. He had won it previously in 1940, when he was only 17 and the youngest ever to win it. That year he also won the Interscholastic and Junior championships for the Maine golf Triple Crown.

When he returned from the war, Lebel attended Bowdoin in 1948 for one year and won the State Intercollegiate championship for the college, and was also New England Amateur runner-up.

Inspired by a beloved uncle who was an oral surgeon, from Bowdoin Lebel went to Tufts Dental School. He graduated from Tufts in 1951 and moved to Portland where he maintained a successful oral surgery practice for many years.

But he never left golf. Described as a having a friendly manner and an infectious grin, golfers who knew him all believed Lebel would have succeeded as a professional golfer if he had not been busy with his other profession. He was popular and always invited to participate in tournaments.

He won a total of six Maine Amateur championships. After his 1940 and 1942 wins in the resident category, he also won the Open Amateur in 1946 and the Combined Amateur in 1958, 1961, and 1965. In 1960 and 1961, he also won the Shawnee Open in Pennsylvania and countless other out-of-state individual and team matches.

Lebel reprised his first win at the Martindale Country Club many times over, by winning a total of 47 club championships, a national record. The first year he was eligible to play as a senior, he won, and won many senior titles after that first one. For 50 years, he was a member of the tri-state golf team.

In 1999, he underwent major heart surgery. When he could no longer play golf, Lebel renewed his interest in playing jazz trumpet, because along with his many other interests, he had played horn in school bands at his high school and at Bowdoin. His skills also included woodworking and framing.

He was inducted into the Maine Sports Hall of Fame and the Maine Golf Hall of Fame, as well as the Lewiston-Auburn Sports Hall of Fame in 1985. Lebel and his wife, Jeanne, were married for 61 years and had seven children. His daughter, Susan Lebel Young, a psychotherapist, wrote a book about her dad called *Lessons from a Golfer*. Lebel died in Falmouth, September 16, 2009.

19

BOB LEGENDRE

Two-Time Olympic Pentathlete

So many overachievers, so little time . . . but Pierre-Robert Lucien "Bob" Legendre was a highly unusual athlete, who really had little time.

"Bob" LeGendre, or Legendre depending on the source, was born in Lewiston, January 7, 1898, the last of ten children in the area of the city known as Little Canada, or The Island. His father, a police officer, died the year after he was born, forcing his mother and older siblings to work in the flourishing cotton mills and related industries.

Bob was able to escape that fate somehow, managing, unlike his siblings, to graduate from Jordan High School. The year he graduated, 1917, was also the year his mother died. Since the family was poor, the athletic prowess he displayed in high school may have earned him athletic scholarship assistance. He spent a year at Hebron Academy, then went on to Georgetown University.

A priest at Georgetown called him "the greatest all-around athlete Georgetown or any college ever had." The 6-foot, 3-inch Legendre excelled at track, and field, but also successfully played basketball, halfback in football, and pitcher in baseball. He settled on the demanding pentathlon, then known as the "classic" for its combination 200-meter sprint, javelin throw, discus hurl, long-jump, and 1500-meter run. At the time, it was considered the most demanding test of an athlete's skill. Jim Thorpe took the gold in the1912 pentathlon and decathlon.

In his freshman year at Georgetown, Legendre helped the university take the pentathlon crown from the University of Pennsylvania for the first time in many years. The 1916 Olympics were canceled because of World War I, so Legendre left school to enlist in the Student Army Training Corps. This allowed him to participate in the Inter-Allied Games in Belgium, a competition between members of the military from Allied nations. The 21-year-old Legendre won first place in the pentathlon.

By 1920, the Olympics were restored and Legendre tied for third place in the pentathlon, but was designated fourth place. He had better success in 1922, when he won the pentathlon in the collegiate championship games for the third year in a row, setting records in the 200-meter run and the javelin throw.

An injury just before the games meant he didn't qualify for the long-jump team. Unfazed, he won the bronze medal in the pentathlon, and during that contest, set the record for the long jump at 25 feet, 5.75 inches.

After earning a PhD and a DDS from Georgetown, Legendre, described as a modest young man, signed a Hollywood movie contract. His acting career never materialized, however, other than a short documentary about some of his 1919 Allied Games athletic achievements.

In the days when amateur athletes earned no money at all from their achievements, his turn toward dentistry no doubt just indicated a career path that would pay the bills. Unfortunately, Legendre contracted pneumonia and died unexpectedly in Brooklyn, New York, on January 21, 1931 at age 33.

Lewiston afforded him a huge hero's welcome after the 1919 Allied Games, with a reception, speeches, and a parade. Local Franco-Americans were proud that he could communicate with the game's hosts in their language. Reportedly, Legendre is the only Maine native selected for the Helms Foundation's American Athlete Hall of Fame. He was inducted into the Maine Sports Hall of Fame in 1980.

His mentor at Georgetown wrote in an obituary that despite all the honors he earned, Legendre told him "the tribute he most enjoyed and appreciated was the banquet given in his home city."

20

WALTER L'HEUREUX

Pitched Five Scoreless Innings Against the
DiMaggio Brothers

Walter L'Heureux was born in Sanford on November 19, 1922, into a Franco-American family that loved baseball. He was one of five brothers who all served in the military and played baseball while in service. Two of the brothers were wounded in action, but all returned to Sanford after World War II and continued to play ball.

Drafted in their teens, the brothers all left for the war at different times, but they were all away during the years between 1941 and 1945, serving variously in Europe, the Pacific, the Philippines, Australia, and Japan. Bob and Henry earned Purple Hearts in France and Italy. Within nine months of entering the service, Walter was promoted to first sergeant, serving in Australia.

Walter, the left-handed pitcher, was a baseball standout. He played ball with the 8th Army Company A Engineers in Australia, where he earned his fame. Playing against his Army team was a Navy All-Star team with a host of major league players that reportedly included both Dom DiMaggio, a Red Sox centerfielder, and his brother, Joe DiMaggio, famed New York Yankees slugger.

In the one game Walter pitched, he allowed only three runs in five innings against the major leaguers, striking out both DiMaggio brothers. However, the Army team manager took L'Heureux out in the sixth inning. The next pitcher gave up nine runs in one inning, causing Army to lose the game.

However, L'Heureux's performance in that game put him in the Maine Baseball Hall of Fame in 1982. DiMaggio was quoted as saying that L'Heureux "had one of the best curve balls I have seen all season."

In these morale-building wartime games the military sponsored, L'Heureux reportedly also played against other famous major leaguers such as Phil Rizzuto, Johnnie Pesky, and Ted Williams.

When he came home after the war, L'Heureux, then 24 years old, pitched for the professional baseball team, the Granby Red Sox in Canada's Border League. He was offered a contract with a New York Yankees team in Geneva, New York, but gave up professional ball to return home to Sanford to raise a family.

He and his wife Christine wed in 1946 and were married for 60 years until she died. They had three children.

L'Heureux and his brothers all returned to Sanford after the Army, where they frequently showed up at the town's Goodall Park, and developed a love of golf. Walter, Art, and Henry were known as the L'Heureux brothers in local baseball lore. The trio played for several local teams during their heyday, such as the Goodall Sanford team, and a group of Sanford Twilight League teams.

Henry, the youngest brother, became a catcher in their youth because Walter, who had been catching, got hit in the eye by a ball and decided not to catch any more. Walter praised his brother as "the best catcher I ever threw to." Henry was inducted into the Maine Baseball Hall of Fame in 2008.

Walter also worked at a shoe company for a while, before becoming a self-employed carpenter. Successive generations of the L'Heureux family continue to play sports in Sanford. Walter died in Sanford on December 18, 2007, at the age of 85.

21

GAIL LIBERTY

Three-Time National Women's Pistol Champion

Gail N. Liberty was born in New Hampshire on February 19, 1938, but her family moved to Auburn in 1945. Her youth was devoted to academics. She graduated as valedictorian of Edward Little High School in 1956, then went on to Boston's New England Deaconess School of Nursing.

A year after her 1959 graduation as a registered nurse, Liberty joined the Air Force as a nurse and made the service a 25-year career. While serving, she also managed to earn a bachelor's degree in nursing, graduating magna cum laude from the University of Pennsylvania. Later, she earned a master's degree from Arizona State University.

Liberty also became a nurse practitioner and primary care physician's assistant, and served in both capacities at Air Force bases around the country and overseas. During the Vietnam War she did a two-year tour as a flight nurse on aerial medical evacuation teams, ferrying wounded servicemen from Vietnam to hospitals around the Pacific and the United States and earning military awards for her service.

That might be enough for a lot of people, but early in her Air Force career, Liberty developed an interest in competitive pistol shooting. Turns out she had a real talent for it and it didn't take long for her to rack up major awards.

She won her first national match at Camp Perry, Ohio, in 1961, shooting in the .22 category, competing against 15 men and 6 women. She came in first in seven contests.

Again in 1962 and 1963, Liberty won national pistol kudos. Competing against male opponents, she tied for first at world championship meets in Cairo, Egypt, in 1962 in the center fire competition and was awarded one of the first Distinguished International Shooter badges. That year she also won the national team championship as part of the Western Air Force area team.

In 1966, she retired from competition, but returned in 1981 to tie for first place in Cairo again, in the world championship matches. She was twice recognized as Air Force Athlete of the year. She continued to win silver and bronze medals in international competitions such as the Pan-Am Games in 1983, in the air pistol, and sports pistol meets.

Liberty planned to compete in the first-ever women's shooting event to be held at the 1984 Olympics in Los Angeles, but prior to the qualifying meets, she was diagnosed with multiple sclerosis (MS). Although she was determined to compete, she couldn't achieve more than fourth place in the five matches due to the effects of the disease, when only two Olympic team places were available.

Even with the muscle spasms caused by MS, Liberty remained in the top ten of national competitors. Four years after her diagnosis, she was named San Antonio Outstanding Woman in Sports.

Besides her shooting awards, Liberty was honored with many Air Force awards that include the Air Medal, the Air Force Commendation Medal with three Oak Leaf Clusters, the National Defense Service Medal, the Vietnam Service Medal with four oak leaf clusters, and the Air Force Longevity Service Award Ribbon with five oak leaf clusters.

In 1987 she was inducted into the Lewiston-Auburn Sports Hall of Fame, and in 1989, she was inducted into the Maine Sports Hall of Fame. All told, she won 22 national and international medals for shooting. Liberty died in an Air Force health care center in San Antonio on September 18, 2006, at age 68.

22

DICK MacPHERSON

Famed Syracuse Football Coach

Richard F. "Dick" MacPherson was born November 4, 1930, in Old Town, the youngest of 12 children. He starred on three sports teams at Old Town High, graduating in 1948, and briefly attended Maine Maritime Academy in Castine.

He went from Castine to the Air Force during the Korean conflict, where he served from 1950 until 1954. From 1954 to 1958, he attended Springfield College where he played offensive lineman on the Redmen football team for three years, a team which remained undefeated in 1956. In his senior year, he was captain. During his football career there, Springfield's record was 22–9–1.

After graduation, he moved around for a few years—coaching freshmen at Illinois, then serving as freshman football coach and head wrestling coach at the University of Massachusetts, and holding three titles at the University of Cincinnati: offensive line coach, freshman grid coach, and defensive coordinator. He also worked as defensive backfield coach at the University of Maryland. MacPherson then went to the National Football League's (NFL) Denver Broncos as an assistant defensive coach for four years, which he said was his favorite professional football experience.

His first head coaching job was at the University of Massachusetts Amherst where he stayed from 1971 to 1977, leading his Minutemen to four Yankee Conference championships. When he left them, they'd earned an overall record of 45–27–1—fifth best in league history—plus 27–8–1 in conference play, and they won the Boardwalk Bowl in 1972. The 45 wins placed his record third in school history. While there, he was twice named New England Coach of the Year.

He returned to the NFL as linebacker coach with the NFL's Cleveland Browns from 1978 to 1980 before leaving to return to the college coaching scene, and the job for which he is best known—head coach of the Syracuse Orange.

MacPherson is remembered at Syracuse as the beloved "Coach Mac," who brought the team back from years of failure, and in his ten years from 1981 to 1990, the team earned a record of 66–46–4. The Orange were undefeated (11–0–1) in 1987 for only the second time ever, for which MacPherson was awarded the Lambert Trophy. That team was fourth in final polls, with a record of 4–1–1 in bowl games, his highest team ranking ever. He was named Coach of the Year by 12 different organizations.

His coaching took the Orange to the Cherry, Sugar, Hall of Fame, Peach, and Aloha Bowls. When he left Syracuse, his total college career record was 111–73–5.

From Syracuse, MacPherson took a job as head coach of the New England Patriots, a team that had performed dismally in previous years. In 1990, the Pats' record was 1–15. Coach Mac improved their performance the first of his two years, but the team slumped again in his second year and he was fired. He once said, "I think I made a mistake leaving Syracuse."

On the Syracuse campus, after his death, he was remembered as a "guy who wore his heart on his sleeve," "charismatic and colorful," a great personality, and an involved community member.

Although he could have been hired by another college, he never returned to coaching. He did return to Syracuse, where he had raised his family and proceeded to do radio commentary for Syracuse football games and color work for TV. He and his wife returned to Maine frequently to a home they owned in Princeton.

Walter Abbott, a former University of Maine coach whose Black Bears played Coach Mac's Syracuse team, said of his close friend, "He was a true Mainer. He never forgot where he was from. Anywhere he went, he spread the good word about the state of Maine and the people of Maine."

And the good word wasn't all. MacPherson sent "CARE packages" to Abbott every year, full of football shoes and helmets for his sons to share with their high school teammates. He would write, "I know those Orono boys can't afford it! "

Abbott also recalled that MacPherson always had a fondness for donuts from LaBree's Bakery in Old Town.

At least seven coaches MacPherson hired as assistants became successful NCAA head coaches. Two of his grandsons, Macky and Cameron, attended Syracuse and played football. One grandson, Macky MacPherson is following in Coach Mac's footsteps. He started as a Kent State running back coach in 2018.

Coach Mac was awarded dozens of honors including honorary doctorates. He was inducted into the Old Town High School Hall of Fame, the Maine Sports Hall of Fame, the Springfield College Athletic Hall of Fame, and the Syracuse Sports Hall of Fame. His biggest honor was his 2009 induction into the College Football Hall of Fame. At that time, he was delighted to say, "I'm the only guy in the state of Maine that's in it."

He died in Syracuse on August 8, 2017.

23

JOHN JOSEPH MAGEE

Legendary Bowdoin College and Olympic Track Coach

John Joseph Magee was not a Maine native, but his 42 years at Bowdoin College certainly qualify him as a Mainer. Magee was a legendary record-breaking track and field coach for the college who also coached four Olympic Teams.

Born in Newark, New Jersey, on January 12, 1883, Magee grew up in East Boston, ran as a sprinter while a student, and briefly coached basketball at Brunswick High School and track for a year at a boys' prep school in Duxbury, Massachusetts, before accepting the job as coach of the Bowdoin track team in 1913, the school's first athletic trainer.

Magee took a year off from Bowdoin in 1918 to train the U.S. Army in France during World War I, where he was wounded. He then survived a trip home across the Atlantic in a vessel that was threatened frequently by German torpedoes.

Upon returning to Bowdoin, he led the team to 20 state championships in 38 years of competition, including a record nine straight wins. In 1920, 1924, 1928, and 1932, the Bowdoin Polar Bears also won the New England Collegiate Championship. Bowdoin also won one Eastern Intercollegiate title.

Magee coached four Olympic teams, and it could have been five. However, in 1936, he lobbied for the United States to boycott the games that would be held in Nazi Germany. When the decision was made to compete in Germany, Magee declined the offer to coach. However, he helped coach teams in the 1920, 1924, 1928, and 1932 Olympics.

During the 1924 summer games in Paris, his most famous Bowdoin athlete, Fred Tootell, class of 1923, won the gold medal in the hammer throw. Tootell went on to serve as a long-time Rhode Island head track coach. Tootell was the first Maine college athlete to win Olympic gold. Magee's other famous athletes included Niles Perkins, U.S. 1940 35-lb. weight throw champion who held the indoor world record for nine years, and Phil Good, who set a record in the 1934 New England high hurdles.

Magee also coached U.S. teams that competed in other international games held in San Francisco and Chicago in 1932 and 1933 in which the United States faced the British, and again in the Far East and Scandinavian countries in 1934 and 1937.

Among his many other accomplishments, Magee helped found the Maine branch of the Amateur Athletic Union (AAU), served as its president, and served as vice president of the national AAU for two years, 1932 and 1933. He was named president of the Association of College Track Coaches of America, and was one of the first coaches inducted into the Helms Foundation Hall of Fame in Los Angeles, a private entity named for its founder. He also served on the advisory board of the New England Intercollegiate Athletic Association.

He was also a longtime member of the Maine State Boxing Commission, helping revise the state's boxing rules. When he retired from coaching in 1955, Bowdoin named Magee emeritus director of track and field and honor member of the Bowdoin College Alumni Council in 1964.

The outdoor, all-weather track at Bowdoin's Whittier Field stadium is named for him—the John Joseph Magee track—as is an eating establishment on campus, "Jack Magee's Pub & Grill." He was inducted into the Maine Sports Hall of Fame in 1977 and the Bowdoin College Athletic Hall of Honor in 2008. Magee married Gladys Thornton in 1911 and they had three children. He died in Brunswick on January 1, 1968, at age 84, just 11 days before his 85th birthday.

24

KEVIN MAHANEY

All-Around Athlete, Olympic Silver Medalist in Sailing

Kevin P. Mahaney is one of those people who seems to do well at whatever he tries, particularly if it's athletic.

Born in Bangor on March 31, 1962, Mahaney grew up an avid skier, apparently good enough at it to make the U.S. ski team in the 1980s.

After graduating from Holderness Prep School in New Hampshire in 1981, he went on to Middlebury College in Vermont, where he joined the lacrosse team. Freshman year, new to the sport, he achieved All-American honorable mention as a goalkeeper. In all, while at Middlebury he was named an All-American, All New England, and All-ECAC.

Mahaney graduated from Middlebury in 1984 with a degree in economics and a minor in physics. In 1987, he earned an MBA with a focus on finance from the University of Chicago Graduate School of Business.

Meanwhile, all along in his off time in the summer, Mahaney was sailing.

By 1988 he was a member of the U.S. sailing team that won five medals at the Olympic summer games in Seoul. In all, he was three times North American champion, three times North American J-24 champion, champion helmsman in classes Star J-35, International One-Design, IMS and IOR, runner up at the Olympic Practice Regatta in 1991, and second in the 1991 European Match Racing Championships.

In 1992, at the summer Olympics in Barcelona, Spain, he skippered the vessel that brought home the silver in the soling event with his partners Jim Brady and Doug Kern. Soling is a sailboat style, introduced to the Olympics in 1972 and retired in 2000.

He announced his retirement from sailing in 1992 at age 30, after only 10 years of professional competition, right after the Mazda World Championship of Match Race Sailing event at Long Beach, California—the same year he was named Rolex Yachtsman of the Year and inducted into the National Sailing Hall of Fame.

But then Mahaney had a change of heart. He decided he wanted to skipper a sailboat in the America's Cup competition in 1995. He and a team formed a group they called PACT 95 (Partners for America's Cup Technology) and commissioned a vessel they called Young America. They raised $18 million for their venture in just 30 months.

The group took a novel approach—depending on computer technology design without building a prototype and ending up with the fastest boat in the American tryouts. Unfortunately, while the team excelled in the challenger series, they lost the last race to former America's Cup winning skipper, Dennis Conner. Under the rules, Conner could choose any of the three American entries and used Young America, because it was the fastest vessel, to race in the finals, but lost to New Zealand.

Another novelty: Mahaney commissioned American pop artist Roy Lichtenstein to paint a mermaid across the boat's hull and a spinnaker with rays of sunlight. The original spinnaker was lost and Mahaney has offered a reward for its return. In 2003, the mermaid hull was given a permanent home at the Storm King Art Center in Cornwall, New York. The hull was also displayed at Mahaney's alma mater, Middlebury in 2017.

After sailing, Mahaney returned to snow sports. He competed in a national championship parallel giant slalom event in 2004 in his age group (over 40) and won. He's competed at regional events sponsored by the USSA (U.S. Ski and Snowboard Association). He expressed a desire to ski on every continent during an around-the-world trip.

In 2005, Mahaney cycled the length of the Tour de France route, 2,241 miles, to raise more than $100,000 for the Lance Armstrong Livestrong and Tyler Hamilton Foundations, devoted to cancer and MS, respectively.

In 1988, he became president and CEO for the Olympia Companies, a real estate company in Portland, Maine. In 1991, he was appointed a trustee of the University of Maine's seven-campus system, chair of the Physical Plant Committee.

Being great at sports is a Mahaney family tradition. In 2000, Kevin was inducted into the Maine Sports Hall of Fame, joining his father Larry (1997), and his uncle Keith (1994). Larry was a basketball, baseball and track star, at Fort Fairfield High School and an all-state basketball star for the University of Maine. Uncle Keith excelled in the same high school sports and was considered one of the best basketball players ever to come out of Aroostook County. He broke records for the University of Maine and had a successful coaching career in basketball, football and golf.

In 2006, he was named a trustee of the U.S. Ski and Snowboard Team Foundation. In 2008, Middlebury College rededicated their arts center as the Kevin P. Mahaney Center for the Arts. He was awarded an honorary Doctor of Law degree from Thomas College in 1996.

There's likely to be a third Mahaney generation in the sports hall of fame: Kevin has three snowboarding sons.

Despite the apparent multigenerational gift for athletics, Mahaney says "There is no such thing as a natural. I'm definitely an analytical guy."

AL McCOY

Fought Joe Louis for the Heavyweight Boxing Title

Have you ever heard of Fleurent Alfred Lebrasseur? No? Perhaps Florian Alfred Lebrasseur? Or Floyd Alfred Labrasseur? If not, but if you're a fan of boxing you might have heard of Al McCoy. Same guy. Even though he lost, he's the only Mainer ever to fight for the world heavyweight title.

Fleurent/Florian Alfred (Floyd A.) "Al McCoy" Lebrasseur was born in Winslow, April 11, 1912, and began competing as an amateur by the age of 13, when he weighed only 97 pounds. He went on to compete in every level of the sport, from flyweight to heavyweight, on a state, regional, national, and international level.

When he chose his ring name, he used his middle name and his mother's maiden name. She was Irish and his dad was French-Canadian. When he became a grown man, his height was 5 foot, 11 inches and his reach 74 inches. His weight varied because he would choose to lose or gain weight to fight in different weight classes, although as an adult, he usually fought as a light heavyweight.

In 1928, when he was just 16, he defeated Mike Marier of Westbrook for the Maine featherweight title.

McCoy was described as having an unorthodox boxing style and being a tough, courageous fighter who lost only 15 decisions in hundreds of fights. His one knockout came at the hands of a 6-foot, 5-inch French fighter, Andre Lenglet in Montreal. Two weeks later in Boston, McCoy evened the score by beating Lenglet badly.

McCoy was also popular in Canada, especially Quebec, and was once designated Canadian light heavyweight champion when he won a tournament in Quebec. He was also popular in Boston. Some writers credited him with keeping the sport alive there during some otherwise lean years.

He faced many formidable opponents, but lost to one of them most likely just because he miscalculated. In 1935, he dropped weight to fight Jock McAvoy in Madison Square Garden as a middleweight. Turned out McAvoy was a light heavyweight. And yet, although McCoy was knocked down in the first round, he bounced back and made McAvoy earn his decision.

McCoy was admired for his tenacity. He won several matches where his opponents outweighed him, including title holders who were light heavyweights and middleweight champions. He never lost on a foul. He fought with seven world champions during his career, defeated four onetime light heavyweight champions. His 1935 defeat of Tony Shucco made him the first Mainer to win the New England heavyweight title.

In 1935, he fought Tommy Loughran of Philadelphia, the undefeated light heavyweight champion of the world from 1927 to 1929, then considered one of the best fighters of all time. McCoy fought him twice in one month, and was one of few fighters to win a decision over "The Phantom from Philly."

Sports writers have written that being from Maine limited the careers of many great state boxers because they were past their prime before they got a shot at the big time, such as McCoy's chance at the world heavyweight title on December 16, 1940. He also served in World War II.

McCoy earned his shot at the title for beating a few big time fighters and losing to a couple of others in disputed decisions the year before the big match. At Boston Garden, McCoy faced Joe Louis, but McCoy was 31 pounds lighter than the reigning champ. The fight was stopped at the end of the fifth round due to McCoy's swollen left eye. The match was called as a TKO in the 6th round.

He lived in many places other than Winslow and Waterville. McCoy moved to Lynn, Mass. where his manager lived, and lived there until 1968. For the next ten years, he and his wife Gertrude lived in Long Island, New York. They ended up in Florida, where McCoy died in 1988, at age 76.

McCoy was inducted into the Maine Sports Hall of Fame in 1984.

CARL "STUMP" MERRILL

From University of Maine to the Yankees

Carl Harrison "Stump" Merrill was born February 15, 1944, in Brunswick. Like so many talented athletes, he played more than one sport. At Brunswick High, he was such an outstanding catcher with a great hitting record, that he was named Maine's number one high school catcher in a newspaper poll. As quarterback, he also led the football team to the 1961 Class B state football championship.

At the University of Maine in Orono, the 5-foot, 8-inch Merrill lettered in football and played for three years, played baseball for four, and earned a degree in physical education. While at the university, he achieved two baseball firsts: playing in the first college World Series for any Maine team and chosen in the first draft pick ever.

His 1964 Black Bears team made it to the 1964 College World Series, where he was the starting catcher—the first Maine school ever to make the series. They won only three games, but those wins ranked them third in the country. In those days, the University of Maine offered no financial aid and the team had to go up against bigger schools that had many scholarship athletes. Enhancing the accomplishment, in addition to being a school of only 10,000 students, the team had nine sophomores. Merrill threw out all 18 runners who faced him.

Merrill was a Maine All-State selection in baseball in 1965 and 1966 as well as an All-Yankee Conference Selection in 1965 and 1966

His coach was Jack Butterfield, who gave him his nickname and his entree to his lengthy career with the New York Yankees. One day in 1963, when Merrill was walking with another player who was 6 feet, 5 inches and Butterfield was calling his name, trying vainly to get his attention, the coach finally yelled, "Hey Stump, you little devil, turn around." It worked and it stuck.

In another first, Merrill was chosen in the first-ever baseball draft of 1965. Before the draft was implemented, Merrill had several offers from individual major league teams while a student. When the draft began, he was chosen by the Minnesota Twins and the Baltimore Orioles in another round. He elected not to leave college, but when he graduated in 1966, he accepted a draft by the Philadelphia Phillies and played in the minor leagues until 1971, when he blew out a knee.

Merrill returned to the University of Maine, where he served as assistant baseball, basketball, and football coach for five years. While he was there, in 1976 the Black Bears made it to the College World Series again, where they won two games.

Meanwhile, his former coach, Butterfield, left the University of Maine for the University of South Florida and went from there to the New York Yankees. In 1977, Butterfield invited Merrill to join the Yankees as a pitching coach in West Haven. After that he was a manager with several Yankees minor league teams, including the Nashville Sounds. Merrill said that as a big country music fan, the Nashville post was "heaven."

During the 1981 baseball strike, the Yankees sent their coaches to minor league teams and Yogi Berra joined Merrill in Nashville. Merrill's record in the minors was impressive enough that he was called to New York for a while in 1985 as Berra's first base coach. He returned in 1986 for a stint as a coach. Four years later he became manager of the New York Yankees. The team was in a slump at the time, and Merrill was quoted as saying, "Usually it's the manager that is the one to go. So you are basically hired to be fired."

He stayed with the Yankees in various capacities besides coaching, including front office duties, roving minor league advisor, and scouting, for more than 40 years. As a minor league manager, Merrill won five league titles, had the best record in the league for his first five years, then a second best, followed by another first. He participated in four Old Timer's Day games with the Yankees and has served as a guest instructor for spring training.

As a college student, Merrill was awarded scholarship funds from the Brunswick Area Student Aid Fun (BASAF). He was the first student ever to repay all the scholarship money he was given, so in 1967 the organization honored him by creating the Carl "Stump" Merrill Award Fund. He also spent some winters as an assistant football coach at Bowdoin College in his hometown of Brunswick. He and his family live in nearby Topsham, across the street from his brother.

Merrill was inducted into the University of Maine Sports Hall of Fame in 1991, not only for his baseball accomplishments but for football and coaching as well. He joined the Maine Baseball Hall of Fame in 1989, the Maine Sports Hall of Fame in 1992, the International League Hall of Fame in 2009 and the Maine Sports Legends Hall of Honors at the University of Maine in 2019.

（27）

CHARLES MILAN III

Maine's Winningest Candlepin Bowler

Charles "Charlie" Milan III is in the middle of a long line of Charles Milans from Brewer. Milan was born July 14, 1936, and began competing at candlepin bowling at 12. He started winning bowling championships in 1951 while a student at John Bapst High School, when he took the Junior State Championship at age 15. He won it again the next year.

In 1955 and 1956, he won his first adult titles while a student at St. Anselm's College in New Hampshire. He took some time off from competition to serve in the military, but he returned to the sport in 1959 to win the Maine State Singles title. After that, he really never stopped. He's a Maine bowling legend.

Milan won the singles title at least 24 times, the New England Championship a few times, a few international titles, and set some state and world records. He holds titles in doubles, mixed doubles, and team events. He helped start the International Candlepin Bowling Association Championship, ran the Charlie Milan and the Bridget Milan Memorial tournaments, and helped start and run the American division of the World Invitational Men's Team Championship Tournament.

His family owns the Bangor-Brewer Bowling Lanes, which he and his wife Marie started in 1962. They were married for 51 years and had four children, including John IV (who has a son named John V). Marie passed away in 2011.

Some of Milan's records still hold. He won an Eastern Maine title in Rockport in 1963 with a 10-string score of 1,467, and a 5-string 707 still holds for his win in the 1968 world tourney.

Milan appeared on and hosted TV bowling shows for the entire duration of the genre. Popular in New England starting in the 1950s in Boston, the original show, "Candlepin Bowling," survived into the 1990s. Winners of each week's matches would return the following week to face opponents who won qualifying matches or "roll-offs" during the week. Appearing on one show, Milan rolled a 460 triple, the highest ever televised.

Milan was an all-around athlete in high school, and despite his many championships in bowling, it's still not his only interest. He went skydiving in his 70s.

In 1982, he was inducted into the Maine Sports Hall of Fame, one of the youngest athletes afforded that privilege and the first male bowler. In 1990, his home city of Brewer issued him a certificate of commendation for winning his 22nd Maine championship title.

He was inducted into the Maine Candlepin Bowling Hall of Fame in 2005, the same year, at age 68, he was runner-up in the Maine State Men's Championship. In 2014, he teamed up with Amanda Carroll of Gray to win the Can-Am mixed doubles tourney against 64 teams, 32 from New England and 32 from Canada's New Brunswick and Nova Scotia provinces.

28

TONY MINER

Two-time All-American at
University of Southern Maine

Anthony F. "Tony" Miner was born February 15, 1975, and grew up in East Winthrop. He attended Cony High School in Augusta where his skills as a third baseman (and sometimes first baseman) and hitter helped the Rams win two Class A State Championships in 1990 and 1991. Cony boasts a "rowdy" student cheering section, known as the "Cony Crazies."

From there, the 6-foot, 2-inch Miner went on the University of Southern Maine (USM), where his right-handed fielding and batting skills again proved valuable. In 1996, he was chosen third baseman for the National Collegiate Athletic Association (NCAA) Division III All-America First Team by the American Baseball Coaches Association. He was a two-time All-American at USM and he was also three-time Division III first team All New England.

In 1997, the NCAA honored Miner with the same All-America First Team distinction again, but that wasn't all. That year, the Huskies won the Division III baseball championship in Salem, Virginia, winning the 15th and final game against the College of Wooster (Wooster, Ohio) 15–1.

That game also allowed Miner to set his Division III record for hits in 35 consecutive games while boasting a batting average of .397. He was also chosen 1997 New England Collegiate Baseball Association Player of the Year in the Little East Conference.

After college, Miner was drafted by the Cleveland Indians organization. He played with their minor league team, the Watertown Indians in New York in 1997, then to the Adirondack Lumberjacks in 1998. There he sustained a career-ending injury.

Miner went from New York to the Savannah Country Day School in Georgia to serve as the prep school's hitting and infield coach for two years, leading the team to their first two state tournaments. He then joined Savannah State University as an assistant coach during 2006 and 2007.

Soon after, he opened the Miner League Baseball & Softball Academy with a partner, a private facility for all ages and skill levels offering camps, clinics, teams, and private lessons. Miner trained more than 60 players who went on to play at college and professional levels in baseball and softball.

The academy also raises funds to support local kids' baseball and softball teams. Miner also taught baseball and softball classes at various schools in the area, and coached 12 (United States Specialty Sports Association) USSSA/Triple Crown State Championship Teams in four age groups in Georgia.

Miner lives with his wife and children in Pooler, Georgia, but in 2019, he returned to Maine for a while to serve as head coach with the Southern Maine River Rats, a winter training program for high school baseball and softball athletes based in Saco. He also coached with the Greater Northeast Collegiate Baseball League, a summer league with six teams that play at various southern Maine fields. More than 40 colleges from Maine to New York send players for training throughout the summer.

29

MARCUS NASH
Two-time Olympian Nordic Skier

Marcus Nash was born April 1, 1971, in Bristol, England. Despite his birthday, his cross-country skiing is no joke. The family of the nine-time U.S. Champion left England for Canada when he was 5 and moved to Maine when he was 7. He was always skiing.

Nash grew up in Fryeburg, where he followed along with his older brother, skiing the snowmobile trails behind their home. He attended Fryeburg Academy, but he had been training with the school's ski team since sixth grade because both his older brother and sister were already team members.

When he entered the high school, he quickly became the number one skier in his freshman year and never lost a cross-country ski competition in Maine. He anchored the winning 16–17-year-old age group at the Junior Olympics in Lake Placid when he was 16. He became U.S. Junior National Champion in 1987, 1988, and 1989, and in 1991 he joined the U.S. World Junior championship team.

In 1989, his senior year, Nash's team was a full minute behind in a relay race, the last event of the 1988 Class A championship held in Rumford. He was the last skier in the 3-K loop of the relay and the competition was more than a minute ahead of the Fryeburg team. When Nash was tagged and skied into the woods, the spectators watched the hill where the skiers would emerge, because the first one out would definitely be the winner. Sure enough, Nash was the first to appear, having gained a minute on the other team in less than 3k.

Nash became an American citizen at 18, and attended the University of Utah on an athletic scholarship. Oddly enough, his coach in Utah was Pat Miller of Mexico, Maine. A member of the Utah ski team from 1992 to 1994, Nash was chosen three times as the Western Athletic Conference Scholar Athlete. In 1993, he became an NCAA All-American. He competed as a member of the World Ski Championship Team in Sweden in 1993, and would do so four more times.

As a member of the U.S. Ski Team, he raced in the Olympics twice, in 1994 in Lillehammer, Norway, and in Nagano, Japan, in 1998. He was chosen for the 1994 team because he performed well in the trials, although he missed the last tryout race, felled by a case of bronchitis.

He won U.S. Championship titles in various distance races nine times between 1997 and 2000. In 2000, Nash raced in the Goodwill Games in Lake Placid where he and a teammate won the Gold Medal in the Cross Country Relay for men, beating the favored Norwegian teams.

During those four years, the 5-foot, 10-inch Nash also twice won the Finlandia Award from the U.S. Ski Association, given to the outstanding skier in the United States. In addition, he won the Mike Gallagher Award five times, which is given to the senior men's overall winner at the U.S. Cross Country Championships, and he won the Gail Cotton Burton Award five times, which is given to the winner of the men's 15-km race at the U.S. Cross Country Championships.

One of the places Nash trained was Truckee in the Lake Tahoe region, where he met his future wife, Katerina Hanusova, a fellow Olympic cross-country skier as well as an Olympic mountain biker. They married in 2005.

In Truckee, Nash coached and mentored local skiers, working as a volunteer for the Far West Ski Association. He helped design the U.S. Ski Team Technique development program and a competition program for Far West Juniors. He represented the United States for a total of eight years, starting in 1994, then retired in 2002 to become a pilot with Cathay Pacific Airlines.

In 2010, Nash was inducted into the Maine Ski Hall of Fame for his achievements as a competitor and his continuing contributions to the sport of cross-country skiing.

"The Olympic Games transcend politics and most of the turmoil in the world. Sharing this experience with my close friends and teammates is something I will always cherish," said Nash.

30

ERIK NEDEAU

Record-Setting Runner and First Maine Student to Break the Four-Minute Mile

Erik "Ned" Nedeau, was born August 30, 1971, in Island Falls, grew up in Kennebunk, and attended Kennebunk High School. Before he graduated in 1989, the young track star had won medals in Junior Olympics in the 400 hurdles and decathlon and six Maine State Championships.

Nedeau set state records in 1989 for the 300-yard indoors and the 400-meter outdoors, and became the first Maine high school student to do the 400 in less than 50 seconds. His high school records in the 300, 400, and 600 meters still hold. He earned his six Maine state titles in those 300-, 400-, and 600-meter races, as well as the triple jump. He earned medals in both the 400-meter hurdles and the heptathlon in the Junior Olympics.

When he went to Northeastern University in Boston, he was coached by longtime coach Mark H. Lech, a seven-time New England conference Coach of the Year, who called Nedeau "one of the most talented athletes to come out of the state of Maine."

Lech became head coach at the University of Maine in 1999. He moved Nedeau up to longer races, the 800 and then 1500 meters. Nedeau soon excelled in those distances as well. He began earning titles in his second indoor season at Northeastern when he won the Greater

Boston and New England 500s. In the next outdoor season, he won the New England and America East 800. He became a five-time NCAA All-American in both.

He also ran individually in NCAA cross-country championship meets. Six times, *Track & Field News* ranked him in the top ten American middle-distance runners for his performances in the 800, the 1500, and the mile.

Nedeau earned 12 New England titles, two IC4A titles (Intercollegiate Association of Amateur Athletes of America), one of the oldest track meets in the country) and placed second at the NCAA Championships in 1994. He set Northeastern University school records in the 800-, 1000-, 1500-meters and the mile.

When Nedeau was at Northeastern, the university was part of the America East Conference. Nedeau's 1:48.51 personal record time in the 800 set at Northeastern is still an outdoor conference record.

At the U.S. Olympic trials in 1992, Nedeau came in seventh in the 800, with a time of 1:46.19, then the fastest time for a New Englander. He won a bronze medal in the 1500 at the World Indoor Championships in 1995, and came in fourth at the 1996 Olympic trials in the 1500.

In 1995, Nedeau had his greatest race at the World Indoor Championships in Barcelona, Spain. He passed several runners during the last 100 meters of the mile race, winning bronze, and finishing just .37 seconds behind Hicham El Guerroui, the world record holder and considered by many to be the world's best-ever middle-distance runner. Nedeau's bronze is the only medal ever won by a Maine man at a world championship.

His last year of indoor college competition, Nedeau won the New England mile with 3:59.6, the fastest by a college student in New England. He was the first person from Maine to break the 4-minute mile. He also won the New England 800, and set the America East indoor record for the mile with a time of 4:04.59.

During his last outdoor season that year he placed third in the U.S. nationals with a 3:38.31 in the 1500, the best time ever for a New England college runner. In addition to titles in the New England 1500, the America East 800 and 1500 and the IC4A 800, he placed second in the NCAA 1500 with 3:42.44, and for the third time, won All-America honors. He was named to several All-America teams and won America East

Track Scholar/Athlete of the Year honors four times. He was also known for wearing black socks.

Nedeau graduated from Northeastern University cum laude in 1994 with a degree in criminal justice and a prestigious scholar/athlete award, then in 1996, earned a master's of science in sports studies from the University of Massachusetts at Amherst.

After graduation, he joined the New Balance Track Club. He came in first in the 1995 U.S. indoor mile and third in the 1995 World Championships. He was also an alternate in the 1500 for the 1996 Olympics. He came in fourth in tryouts, and missed making the Olympic team by six-hundredths of a second.

In 1995, he also joined the coaching team at Amherst College as assistant track and field coach. In 1997, he was named interim head coach, and then given the job permanently. He helped the school's athletes break 22 varsity and freshman records, while producing five All-Americans, six NCAA qualifies, and several more winners. He stayed 20 years, elevating the men's and women's programs to higher accomplishments than ever before. In 2007, he coached Amherst's first-ever national champion cross-country team. In 2007, he was installed in the U.S. Track, Field and Cross-Country Coaches' Association and the National Women's Cross Country Coach of the Year.

Altogether, Nedeau led the Amherst men's and women's teams to four NCAA championships, 73 All-American performances, two Junior National medals, and a number of New England, NESCAC and ECAC championships before he resigned in 2017.

He continued to compete, winning a relay and setting a world age group record in the 4 × 800 meter relay in 2012, with three team members in New York City. That same year, at the Greater Boston Track Club Invitational, he was the masters winner in the mile with a time of 4:21.16. USA Track & Field New England named him Athlete of the Month for January 2013.

Nedeau was inducted into the Maine Running Hall of Fame in 2008 and the Northeastern University Hall of Fame in 2001.

(31)

FREDDY PARENT

Helped the Red Sox Win the 1903 World Series

Alfred "Freddy" Parent Jr. was either 5 feet, 5 inches or 5 feet, 7 inches, and 145 or 155 pounds depending on the account, when he aspired to play professional ball. "Everybody pretty nearly told me I was too small to play baseball and that I would never make a player anyhow," said Parent. Fortunately, he ignored the critics and from an amateur team in Sanford in 1898, he went to a minor-league New Haven team in the Connecticut League.

Parent propelled the Connecticut team to a second-place finish with his .326 batting average, one of the league's best that year. His second year with the team, he helped win the 1899 Connecticut League championship, finishing with a .349 batting average, second in the league, and 76 runs, third in the league. After a year as shortstop with the Providence Grays in the Eastern League, where he dazzled audiences with his 23 stolen bases, 21 doubles, six triples, and four home runs, he was signed with the Boston Americans.

Born November 25, 1875, in the textile town of Biddeford, oldest of a Franco-American family of ten who spoke French as their first language, Parent quit school at 14 to work in a harness shop. He then moved to Sanford at age 16 to work in a textile mill. But baseball was always the first love of the right-handed hitter who played on town lots with a team he helped organize. When he became a backup player for Sanford's semi-pro team, he was spotted by the New Haven team. He had a brief stint with the St. Louis Perfectos, who returned him to New Haven following injuries.

By joining the Boston Americans in 1901, the team that was renamed the Red Sox in 1908, he became historically the first shortstop for the Red Sox. Boston fans loved the scrappy little shortstop for his hustle and dependable hitting. Parent earned a .306 batting average the first year, along with 36 extra base hits. His batting style was to crowd the plate, exposing himself to being hit by pitches—which he was, frequently. In the first ten years of the American League, Parent had the dubious distinction of being sixth in the number of times hit by pitches, often to the head. In those days, fans contributed to injuries by hurling empty bottles rather than paper cups at players on the field. In his second year, Parent's batting average dropped to .275, but he hit 31 doubles, his career record, and led the league with 492 assists.

It was the third year with the Americans that cemented Parent's place in baseball history. That year the Americans won the American League pennant and the first World Series. In the Series, Parent outplayed the then legendary Honus Wagner of the Pittsburgh Pirates, by besting Wagner's series batting average by almost 60 points. Even though Parent was considered one of the "youngsters" on the team, he was an important hitter in the series, who played in all eight games and hit .290, with nine hits and four RBIs in 31 at bats.

One writer said of his performance: "two-way standout Parent made several sparkling plays—cutting off a half-dozen hits with great plays." He ended the series with 28 assists, and a record for the most runs scored—eight—not beaten until Babe Ruth a quarter of century later. Parent ended a total of four no-hit attempts by scoring the only hits for his team in the games.

In 1904, Parent helped propel the Americans to another pennant. He batted .291, scored 85 runs, and four home runs. Admired most for his fielding skills, Parent's stats didn't reflect his performance, according to a *Washington Post* sports writer in 1904, who wrote: "But fielding averages really do not demonstrate the value of any player, for there is Fred Parent, probably the foremost shortstop in the country, occupying a position next to last." He is credited with saving Cy Young's perfect pitching game in 1904 against the Philadelphia Athletics with a brilliant defensive play, one of the four no-hitters he blocked.

Parent played with the Americans until 1907, when he was traded to the Chicago White Sox. Although his performances had begun to decline a bit, some attribute his trade to his constant battles with management—when he demanded and usually got more money. In 1911, he locked horns over pay with Chicago owner Charles Comiskey, who sold him to the Baltimore Orioles of the International League. It was not Siberia, for Parent used the time to perfect coaching skills and make friends with a 19-year-old George Herman "Babe" Ruth, signed by the Orioles in 1914.

The first to earn the "iron man" designation for playing 413 consecutive games from 1901 to 1903, Parent ranked high in the American League's first decade with second in games played and at bat, fourth in hits and sacrifice hits and sixth in total bases, despite many injuries including concussions.

His many other baseball credits include playing for an International League Toronto team and working as player-manager of the Springfield Massachusetts Eastern League team in 1918. He took a coaching job with a Lewiston team in the New England League in 1919, went on to coach at Colby College from 1922 to 1924, then served as Harvard University junior varsity coach from 1926 to 1928. He returned to Maine and managed a baseball club at Goodall Field, where his buddy Babe Ruth played an exhibition game in 1919. Ruth returned to Sanford many times to go fishing with Parent at Sebago Lake.

Throughout his career, he was married to his childhood sweetheart, the former Fidelia LaFlamme. He proposed when she was 16, they married in 1896 and had one son, Fred Jr. They were together for 67 years. Parent was awarded a Lifetime Pass by the American and National leagues in 1936 for his service to the game. In 1960, he appeared on the popular live TV show "What's My Line" with Pittsburgh Pirate Tommy Leach, as two of the participants in the first World Series.

In 1923, his old rival Honus Wagner, shortstop for the Pirates in 1903, said, "Fred Parent is a great ballplayer who never got all the credit he deserved. He was so graceful he made hard plays look easy. I think Parent is the greatest shortstop I ever saw in starting and finishing double plays. As a runner, he excelled in breaking up the double-play ball, and he was a good hitter as well. He had a great throwing arm and could peg the ball from any position as accurately as a bullet shot from a rifle. Parent was especially good at tagging out base runners when they slid."

When he died in Sanford in 1972 at the age of 96, Parent was the last remaining player from the 1903 Red Sox World Series game.

32

JULIE PARISIEN

U.S. Champion Skier, Hall of Famer, and Olympian

Julie Madelein Josephine Parisien was born in Montreal, Quebec, on August 2, 1971, but her parents—both doctors—moved the family to Auburn a year later. There, the Parisiens spent a lot of time skiing at Lost Valley, and became the first family of Maine skiing.

Julie was on skis at age two. She said she really didn't love it then, but she liked the lodge and the hot chocolate. All that turned around when she was seven and started racing her two older brothers down the slopes of Lost Valley. She loved competing. The family also skied weekends at Sugarloaf Mountain.

Lost Valley was like their babysitter, Parisien said. The siblings cut loose on the mountain and mostly concentrated on having fun. She recalled once when her brother hit a jump, caught air, kept going, and landed on a parked car.

Her two older brothers, J. P. and Robbie, went off to Vermont's Burke Mountain Academy, and she followed in their footsteps, graduating in 1989. As a kid, she put posters of ski champions on her wall and told herself she could do what they did. By 13, she had a serious interest in competitive skiing and the talent for it.

In 1989, she won the U.S. Junior Olympic Super G and Giant Slalom titles, and a bronze medal at the World Junior Championships in the

Super G. The next year, she took the combined U.S. title for downhill and slalom. She was a quadruple threat, capable of successfully competing in all four technical Alpine events: slalom, giant slalom, super giant slalom (super-G), and downhill.

At age 19, she won the World Cup giant slalom, the first U.S. woman to do so in six years. It was a thrilling race because Parisien was in 22nd place when she roared down the Mt. Tecumseh trail in Waterville Valley, New Hampshire, to win by a full second.

The year 1991 was a good year; in addition to the giant slalom, she won races at the NorAm, Europa Cup, and other World Cup events within a four-week period. She was named to the Olympic Team for the 1992 Albertville games.

In 1992, the powerful, 5-foot, 8-inch Parisien won a World Cup slalom in Sweden, and the opening 1993 World Cup slalom in Park City. Again that year, she was U.S. combined champion and took a silver medal at the World Championships in Japan. However, in the Olympics she was recovering from a serious collision with a skier a month prior to the races. She was skiing with 13 stitches in her lower lip and four temporary teeth from that encounter. She was also wearing a cast on her broken left wrist after banging into a gate pole a few days after the collision. She came in fourth, "the worst place in the Olympics," said Parisien. Despite her injuries, she missed a medal by only 0.05 seconds.

She went into the 1993–1994 season with the number one ranking in the world in slalom. Unfortunately, a tragedy occurred that would change the family and Julie's career. Her beloved older brother, J. P. (Jean Paul) was killed when a drunk driver forced him off the road. Julie said his death ruined her skiing career. She had won three World Cup races in three seasons before the tragedy, but her standing fell after that.

She took the rest of the 1994 World Cup season off and considered leaving the sport. Instead, she joined the women's North American pro tour, which she dominated for three years. She returned to amateur competition to make the 1998 Olympic Team, placing 13 in the Nagano slalom. She won her third U.S. combined title and a fourth U.S. career championship that year. She retired after the 1998 Olympics.

Her older brother by a year, Rob, and her younger sister by a year, Anne-Lise, also competed in the Olympics as alpine skiers. Jean Paul had been Williams College ski team captain and a coach at Burke Mountain

Academy. Julie was educated at University of Maine in Farmington, the University of Southern Illinois, and the University of Southern Maine.

After her ski career, she and her husband, a doctor, moved to Maine. Julie earned a degree in nursing, coached junior racers at Lost Valley, participated in ski workshops and clinics. They have four children and the family lives in Lewiston.

She was inducted into the Maine Sports Hall of Fame in 2001, the U.S. Ski and Snowboard Hall of Fame and Museum in 2006, and the Maine Ski Hall of Fame in 2008.

33

DOROTHY "DOT" PETTY

Bowler Extraordinaire and First Woman in the Maine Sports Hall of Fame

A native of Portland, Maine, Dorothy "Dot" Petty's career in candle-pin bowling spanned more than 20 years and included 84 titles and 16 records. Her career began in 1965, and in 1978 she was the first woman inducted into the Maine Sports Hall of Fame, which was the second year she won worlds singles' best. The first was in 1967, and in 1969 she achieved a "grand slam" winning singles and women's doubles, mixed doubles and women's teams.

Described as "no bigger than a pint of cider," from 1973 through 1976 Petty was reigning world champion. In 1969, she was women's doubles winner with Peg Nixon. She was all events winner in 1972. She won ten other world titles on teams that included Nixon, Herb McBride, and other partners. She held the state champion title for 10 years from 1969 through 1979, and took it back in 1981.

Candlepin bowling was little known outside of New England, and as one wag said about having to explain it to those ten-pin bowlers from other parts of the country, "In New England we don't call it candlepin, it's just bowling!" With tenpins that are distinctly narrower than the more widespread ten-pin style, candlepin employs smaller balls, making it harder to knock them down, so bowlers get three rolls per "box" (unless they roll spares or strikes).

Petty was Pro Tour Bowler of the Year for four years—1977, 1978, 1982, and 1983—with the World Candlepin Bowlers Congress, an organization based in Massachusetts. She also won two tour stops in 1972 and 1983. In Western Maine title competitions, Petty won 26 championships in five categories.

Her many titles cover 22 bowling categories. She bowled on television, when candlepin bowling was wildly popular with Saturday morning viewers. One show, "Candlepin Bowling," aired from 1961 to 1996. Portland's Channel 13 also hosted a bowling show, where Petty was a frequent attraction and set a record of 28 straight wins in 1968–1969. She set a TV record with a single of 171. The top score possible in candlepin is 300 points per game, but it has never been achieved. Only two people have achieved the record score of 245.

Scarborough's Big 20 Lanes were Petty's home base, where the TV cameras often recorded the action. During one long, tense world championship tournament, Petty was flailing and her fans feared the worst. However, Dot was known for her ability to perform under pressure, just after the clock struck midnight, she rallied, threw a strike on her last roll, and won the championship.

Petty holds seven Maine ten-string records, including one for a state title match in 1975, when she rolled a 1,320. She also recorded state lane high scores in six different bowling alleys from Waldoboro to Biddeford. She was briefly a commentator on a TV show broadcast out of her Big 20 home lanes. In 1985–1986, she was Maine Pro Tour champion and Pro Bowler of the Year. Then she retired. Long on talent but short on ego, Petty reportedly donated all 400 of her title trophies.

(34)

MARK PLUMMER

Always the Amateur, Always the Champion

Mark Plummer of Manchester, is a highly decorated Maine golfer who has won title after title, been inducted into halls of fame, and yet seems to be best known for a match he didn't win.

In 1995, Plummer, then a 43-year-old liquor salesman, played in the U.S. Amateur at the Newport, Rhode Island, Country Club, and made it to the 18th hole of the semi-final match before losing to the19-year-old rising star, reigning U.S. Amateur champion and holder of three consecutive U.S. Junior titles, Stamford sophomore Tiger Woods.

Even that loss was a victory of sorts. No one expected the rumpled "rugged redhead" from Maine, with his "substance over style" approach to the game to survive until the end against the well-groomed wunderkind. But survive he did, garnering nationwide press in the process.

Bespectacled, sporting tousled hair, and his signature thick mustache, a *Golf Journal* writer described Plummer as looking like "a rock music critic held over from the 1960s." Reporters also loved to describe his twisting swing, hunched stance, and unorthodox grip.

Back in his home state, Plummer had enjoyed fame for decades—fame that would have endured without a brush with Woods. Born in 1952, Plummer began his career at around six years old when his dad,

Stan Plummer, lost his temper during a match and broke a 4 iron golf club. Instead of tossing it, he had it re-gripped and presented it to little Mark, who pretty quickly became hooked on golf. The Manchester family's home course was the Augusta Country Club, where Mark set a course record of 60 that still stands.

Maine being Maine, the golf season is short. During the winter, Mark used the enforced break to play high school basketball. He has said he thinks it kept him from burning out on golf.

While he was a student at Hall-Dale High School, Mark and his dad won the 1969 Maine State Golf Association (MSGA) Father/Son Championship. That same year, Mark also won the MSGA Junior title.

At the University of Maine, Plummer led the Black Bears to the 1974 Yankee Conference championship and won himself an All-American honorable mention. In 1979, he won the Bangor Open.

Plummer shows no sign of slowing down, so his list of accomplishments is, by necessity, partial.

Through 2019, Plummer had won 13 Maine and two New England amateur championships. In 2019, he won his sixth Maine Senior Amateur title, a state record. His 13 state amateur championships are also a record. He holds four Maine State Mid-Amateur titles (25 to 55 years old) and a Maine State Match Play title. The former sheriff's deputy also won 11 Bangor Daily News Amateur titles, formerly the Paul Bunyan tournament. He won the 1982 Casco Bay Open with a course record of 62. He also won the 1981 State of Maine championship, an open event, and holds 18 August Country Club championships. In 1982 and 1983, he finished in the top 64 of the U.S. Amateur.

His career has spanned more than 28 years so far, and Plummer is the most decorated Maine golfer ever.

In 1990, Plummer was inducted into the University of Maine Sports Hall of Fame.

When he was also inducted into the Maine Sports Hall of Fame in 1997, the statement read, "Mark Plummer stands unapproached and unmatchable for accomplishments as a Maine amateur golfer."

Brian Bickford, executive director of the Maine State Golf Association, said, "Mark Plummer is Maine golf. He has a swing that's all his own with a personality and grit unparalleled in Maine. His ability to focus on the task and maximize the result no matter what he is faced with is unique to him. His respect for the game earns him the admiration of all who play in our great state."

Unwilling to give up his amateur status, when he was asked to do a commercial featuring him and a Maine lighthouse, he asked the U.S. Golf Association for permission, but the organization unfortunately said he must turn it down even though there was no pay involved.

35

JAY RAMSDELL

Youngest Commissioner in Professional Sports

Jay Ramsdell was a child prodigy, but not of the usual sort. Usually youngsters are considered prodigies if they manifest an early ability to play music, sing, do math, or perform athletic feats. Ramsdell didn't specialize in any of these—rather, he fell in love with basketball and learned everything he could about the game, the statistics, how to do play-by-play, and sports writing.

Born in Bar Harbor, January 30, 1964, Ramsdell grew up loving all sports. By 14, he was a sports writer for the *Bar Harbor Times*. He did that for three years, and served as sports editor for his high school newspaper in 1982. Family and friends described him as an "old soul." He insisted on wearing a suit and tie for school pictures when he was in third grade. He started a regional newsletter for New England Patriots fans in seventh grade, then another for the Red Sox.

Ramsdell did play sports when he attended Mount Desert Island High School. He played baseball and was starting first baseman and captain during senior year. He graduated in 1982, but before that, he covered Hancock County sports for the *Bangor Daily News* from 1979 to 1980. He also did color and statistics announcing for his high school football for a local radio station from when he was 12 until he was 17.

Ramsdell added play-by-play announcing for the same station, covering high school football from 1980 to 1981.

When Ramsdell was 14, a team belonging to the Continental Basketball Association (CBA) came to Bangor. Ramsdell interviewed the owner for a high school newspaper story, and impressed the man so much he asked Jay to help out on opening night. He was assigned to the scorer's table, achieved statistical crew chief status before the end of the night, and was appointed director of public relations for the team before the first week was out.

For his whole high school career, Ramsdell served as director of public relations for the Lumberjacks and by senior year, served as administrative assistant to the league. The team's final season in Maine coincided with his high school graduation, so upon graduation, at 18, his mother drove him to Philadelphia in a red pickup so he could go to work at the CBA headquarters as the league's administrative assistant. Within a year, he was director of operations.

A year later, Ramsdell returned to Bangor to serve as general manager of CBA's new Maine Windjammers. The team only survived one season, so at age 20, Ramsdell returned to the CBA in Denver to become Deputy Commissioner of the CBA, although observers say he really ran the league, not the commissioners.

Four years later, the commissioner, Mike Storen, resigned. Ramsdell was appointed to fill the position. At age 24, he was the youngest commissioner in the history of professional sports, renowned for his knowledge, his passion, his work ethic, and his talent for mimicry. He also had a vision for the CBA that none doubted he could accomplish.

"Everybody loved him," said the owner of a CBA team. Despite his youth, he was respected because he had been with the league for a long time and was clearly not using the CBA as a stepping stone.

In 1989, he appeared on the Today Show and was honored as Sportsman of the Week. Three months later, on July 19, 1989, Ramsdell and the CBA deputy commissioner, Jerry Schemmel, were flying from Denver to the player draft in Columbus, Ohio, on United Airlines Flight 232. The plane lost all its hydraulics and crashed in Sioux City, Iowa. Of the 296 people on board, Ramsdell was one of 111 passengers killed. Schemmel survived.

"In short, he was the CBA's Whiz Kid, the aggressive young leader who was going to take the league to the promised land," said one sports writer. "It was all he ever wanted"

The CBA named their league championship trophy for him in 1989. The nonprofit Jay Ramsdell Foundation was created in his name to provide scholarship assistance to Maine high school seniors, and some nonacademic community groups.

In 2014, he was inducted into the Mount Desert Island Hall of Fame for his contributions to the baseball team and all this other sports activities while a student. He was named "Most Inspirational Player" for the baseball team in his senior year. In 2019, he was inducted into the Maine Basketball Hall of Fame as a "legend of the game."

36

JEAN L. ROY

Bowdoin Hockey Great from Lewiston

Many of Maine's top athletes come from Lewiston and hockey player Jean L. Roy is one of them. Roy started high school at St. Dom's in Auburn, where he was an All-State first team selection in 1978. Roy transferred to Tabor Academy in Marion, Massachusetts, where he earned team Most Valuable Player twice for the Seawolves.

Then Roy returned to Maine to attend Bowdoin College, a school with a long hockey heritage and a strong connection to Lewiston hockey players and coaches. During his freshman year, Roy won First-Team All-New England honors for the 1980–1981 season, was named Eastern College Athletic Conference (ECAC) Rookie of the Year and First-Team All-ECAC. The ECAC is one of six conferences competing in the NCAA Division 1.

That was just the beginning. The competitive Polar Bear freshman also scored eight goals, tying the school record for a defenseman. He broke that record in his sophomore year when he scored 12 goals, and again in his senior year when he scored 11 goals.

Roy set a lot of records at Bowdoin and many of them still stand, decades after his 1984 graduation. Starting in his sophomore year, he won All-American honors. He accomplished that feat a total of four times, the first Bowdoin player ever to do it. In his senior year, he was named outstanding college defenseman for New England, from all divisions by the New England Hockey Writers Association. He was also an East-West All Star who was invited to try out for the 1984 Olympic team.

He is the 10th all-time leading scorer for the Polar Bears, holds the Bowdoin record for career assists with 95, most single-season assists with 35, most career goals with 38 and points, 133, by a defenseman. For a subdivision 1 school, it's a big deal that Bowdoin had any finalists for the Hobey Baker Award for the outstanding player in college hockey. Bowdoin's had two on the list. Jean Roy was a runner-up in 1984.

After graduation, Roy played professional hockey with the Eindhoven Kemphanen in Eindhoven, The Netherlands, a team in the highest-level division in the country.

In 1999, Roy was inducted into the Auburn-Lewiston Sports Hall of Fame, and in 2004 he was inducted into the Bowdoin College Athletic Hall of Honor. He lives in Massachusetts with his wife, Catherine, and their two children.

"He still is arguably the best defenseman ever to wear the black and white jersey," said his Bowdoin coach, Terry Meagher "Who knows where he would be in today's game? Just his skill set. He had a huge shot. Very strong physically in the upper body. But mostly his compete level. All the great ones have that."

ANDREW SOCKALEXIS

Maine's First Great Runner

Andrew Sockalexis, a member of the Penobscot Nation, was born on Indian Island January 11, 1892. He was a gifted runner who started running at age 10, encouraged by his father who built him a track. His father, Francis, was a noted athlete on the island, who excelled in the Penobscot's annual traditional five-hour race. His grandfather was a chief of the Bear Clan.

Early on, Andrew wanted to be a marathon runner, so in addition to the track, he ran all over the island on trails he found. He ran all year round, including on the frozen river around the island where he would run in spiked shoes. He was once timed by a trainer at 13 minutes for a 2.7 mile distance.

He attended Old Town High School, but like many Indian athletes of the day, he was sent to the Carlisle Indian School where he ran track. There's a record of him winning a 5-mile race in Bangor in 1911, but Sockalexis's first serious competitive race was the 1911 Boston Marathon when he was only 18 years old. He finished 17th in a field of 127, with a time of 2:48:45.

In 1912, the Olympics were scheduled in Stockholm, but first Sockalexis ran the Boston Marathon again. Most of the roads of the 24-mile route from South Framingham to Boston were dirt, which turned to mud in the rain. This time, running in mud, he worked his way to the lead only to be passed in the last two miles by Mike Ryan, a New Yorker who set a record that day with his win of 2:21:18, only 34 seconds ahead of Sockalexis. His second-place finish assured Sockalexis a spot as one of the 12 members of the Olympic team.

He was a member of Boston's North Dorchester Athletic Association team, which sponsored the U.S. Olympic team. For the Olympic tryouts at Harvard, Sockalexis trained with a University of Maine track coach. He always told the press he was running for the United States, but also for his Penobscot people.

Sports writers dubbed the 5-foot, 8-inch runner the favorite to win the Olympic marathon, held on a 90-degree day in Stockholm. The plan was for him to hold back until late in the race, because Sockalexis was known for his endurance and effortless style. He apparently held back for too long however, placing fourth with 2:42:07, just seconds behind the third-place runner. A Boston sports writer said he finished strong "like the champion he should have been."

At home, he was greeted like a champion, the first Mainer to participate in the Olympics and to achieve international status in running, and still one of the greatest Maine runners of all time.

Also in 1912, he ran and finished second in a 19-mile race from Old Town to Maplewood Park in Bangor, against his friend Clarence De-Mar, seven-time winner of the Boston Marathon.

In 1913, Sockalexis ran the Boston Marathon again, this time with the added pressure from at least one Boston newspaper, the *Boston Evening Transcript*, which sported a headline: Win, or Lose Her Hand." His fiancee, Pauline Shay, had threatened to end their engagement unless he won. He came in second but she married him anyway.

This time, Sockalexis used the same tactic to start slow and speed up near the end, but again he waited too long and couldn't catch the leader, Fritz Carlson of Sweden, who beat him by two minutes. Sockalexis's time was 2:27:12.

When Sockalexis returned to Indian Island, he continued to run although never again in a marathon. Also in 1913, Sockalexis was diagnosed with tuberculosis, or consumption, a common disease at the time. In 1916, while suffering from a bad cold and chest pains, he ran a 15-mile race from Old Town to Bangor even though his doctor warned

him not to. This time he stayed ahead of the other runners from the beginning and won the race, beating Clarence DeMar. When he finished
running, he coughed up blood and collapsed.

He was sick for a few years, and died at age 27 on August 26, 1919,
in South Paris.

Andrew is related to Louis Sockalexis, the Penobscot who was the
first Native American to play professional baseball. Some accounts say
Louis was his brother, others his first or second cousin. Either way, two
of Maine's major, outstanding athletes are members of the same family,
from the same nation on Indian Island.

When he died, the U.S. Olympic Committee donated a headstone to
his family engraved "A Member of the American Olympic Team at the
Fifth Olympiad held in Stockholm, Sweden, in July, 1912."

In his honor, the Penobscot Nation sponsors an annual Andrew Sockalexis 5 Kilometer Road Run. In November 2019, at the start of Native
American Heritage Month, the Penobscots opened the 1.5 mile Andrew
Sockalexis Training Trail on Indian Island, marked by signs every quarter of a mile depicting his career.

His descendant Michael Sockalexis started and coached an Indian
Island team in the 1970s called the "Andrew Sockalexis Track Club." In
the 1980s, the Penobscot Nation dedicated a new arena on the island
and named it the Sockalexis Ice Arena, to honor Andrew and Louis.
Today it houses the huge Bingo operation run by the Penobscots.

In 1984, he was inducted into the Maine Sports Hall of Fame, and
was a charter inductee into the Maine Running Hall of Fame in 1989,
and the National American Indian Hall of Fame in 2001.

The 124th Maine Legislature honored Sockalexis in 2009 with a joint
resolution on the 90th anniversary of his "untimely" death, to "honor
him as one of Maine's great athletes, who brought much pride to the
Penobscot Nation and to all the people of Maine."

38

LOUIS SOCKALEXIS

First to Break the Major League Color Barrier

Although he's rarely credited with breaking the color barrier in professional baseball, 50 years before Jackie Robinson became the first African American to sign with a national team, Louis Sockalexis from Maine's Penobscot Nation was the first minority player signed with a professional team. He also had the team named for him.

Sockalexis, from Indian Island, Maine, signed with the then Cleveland Spiders in 1897. Reported to be a lightning-like pitcher, an amazing hitter, and an incredibly fast runner, Sockalexis also stole a lot of bases (six in one game). Sportswriter Harry Grayson said Sockalexis was faster than Ty Cobb, a better outfielder than Tris Speaker, and stronger than Babe Ruth. A former Yankee general manager, Ed Barrow, called him "the best hitter, the best thrower, the best fielder, and also, the best drinker." This last "best" was his unfortunate downfall.

Louis Francis Sockalexis was born October 24, 1871, on Penobscot Indian Island Reservation, near Old Town, Maine, son of Francis Sockalexis, a logger, and Frances Sockbeson Sockalexis. His father served as governor of the Penobscot Nation and his grandfather was Chief of the Bear Clan.

Although his father was also considered an excellent athlete, Louis grew to be muscular, nearly 6 feet tall and was considered the best athlete in the tribe, winning all kinds of events from footraces to throwing contests. He and his father entertained local crowds by playing catch across the Penobscot River, some 600 feet.

He loved baseball, and played with semi-pro teams around the state after high school. While playing for one of these, a teammate urged Sockalexis to enroll at the College of the Holy Cross in Worcester, Massachusetts.

At Holy Cross on scholarship, Sockalexis excelled at track—winning five events in a single meet—starred as a running back on the football team, but broke records as a college baseball player, including the world record for the longest throw in baseball, 138 feet.

Former Giants manager John Ward saw him play for Holy Cross and told the magazine *Sporting Life* that "I unhesitatingly pronounce him a wonder. Why he has not been snapped up before by some League club looking for a sensational player is beyond my comprehension."

He stayed only two years at Holy Cross, batting over 400 each season. He is still ranked as one of the nine all-time greatest players for the school. He was being looked at by professional teams when he transferred to Notre Dame University in Indiana, where he stayed only a few months before he was kicked out after brawling at a local bar.

Sockalexis was recruited by the Cleveland major league team then known as the Spiders, but in those days, team nicknames changed frequently. In 1897, local sportswriters began calling the team "Tebeau's Indians" after manager Patsy Tebeau and Sockalexis. The team later came to be known as the Naps after a good player, but it was not until 1914 that the team officially acquired the name Cleveland Indians, reportedly to honor Sockalexis.

When he showed up for training in 1897, Sockalexis wowed his teammates and coaches, and won the starting right field spot. After 20 games, his presence had increased attendance for two reasons: His novelty and reputation as a player attracted fans, but his ethnic derivation also attracted racists who hurled insults at the rookie.

As *Sporting Life* writer Elmer Bates wrote that year, "He is hooted and bawled at by the thimble-brained brigade on the bleachers. Despite this handicap, the red man has played good, steady ball, and has been a factor in nearly every victory thus far won by Tebeau's team."

Besides the racial slurs, fans of the team also yelled "Sock 'em" at Sockalexis. He was also accomplished at gymnastic feats and entertained teammates and fans with his antics. The *Cleveland Plain Dealer* reported that he "occasionally breaks out with some caper that would tear the ordinary man in two."

Unfortunately, Sockalexis brought his drinking problem with him. Just months after joining the team, he got drunk and fell or jumped out of the second-story window of a brothel and sprained his ankle. Five days after the injury he returned to play, but had to be pulled from the game because he was visibly drunk and messing up plays. The team owner suspended him for a few months, but he appeared to clean up his act, and ended the first season with a .338 average and 16 stolen bases.

The following year, he lost his starting position and spent a lot of time on the bench. In 1899, the Cleveland owner bought the St. Louis Browns and did not transfer Sockalexis to the Browns with all the Cleveland team's other star players, The Cleveland team went on to have the worst season in the history of major league baseball. Sockalexis had a relapse during the season and barely played, and when he did, he actually fell down on the field due to his drunken condition. He was released by the team and never played in the major leagues again. He had 367 at bats in the major leagues and ended the three years with a career batting average of 313.

After this, he had a mixed record with semi-pro teams until 1900 when, for two years, he was reportedly homeless, vagrant, often arrested for public drunkenness and disturbances, and spent some time in jail. In 1902, he spent a season playing in Lowell, Massachusetts, a New England League team. Briefly, he joined a Bangor team the next year, which marked the end of his career in organized baseball.

When he returned to Indian Island, he played for town teams, coached youngsters, ran a ferry boat, and went logging in the Maine woods. Although he may have stopped drinking, he was sickly. On Christmas Eve of 1914, he suffered a massive heart attack while cutting down a large pine tree and died. He was 42.

Sockalexis played only 97 major league games, during his short, intense life and career, but the year he died, a teammate paid homage to him in a *Cleveland Leader* interview. Ed McKean, shortstop for the Cleveland team, said, "He was a wild bird. He couldn't lose his taste for firewater. His periodical departures became such a habit [that] he finally slipped out of the majors. He had more natural ability than any player I have ever seen, past or present."

In 2000, Sockalexis was voted into the American Indian Athletic Hall of Fame. During his career he was dubbed variously by sportswriters as the "Deerfoot of the Diamond" and "Chief of Sockem." He was inducted into the Maine Sports Hall of Fame in 1985. Ed Rice is a writer from Orono who published a biography of Sockalexis in 2003, titled *Baseball's First Indian, Louis Sockalexis: Penobscot Legend, Cleveland Indian*. Rice launched an effort in 2015 to raise money to erect a statue to Sockalexis in the Bangor area.

For now, visitors wishing to honor him can only visit his grave on Indian Island. In 1934, the state of Maine replaced the original wooden cross with a stone grave marker emblazoned with a baseball and crossed bats.

(39)

ABBY SPECTOR
Among Maine's Most Successful Golfers

Probably the only reason Abigail L. "Abby" Spector isn't the longest-running world champion pro women's golfer is a medical diagnosis she received at the age of 22.

The Waterville resident had been tearing up the amateur golf scene for years—she was seven-time winner of the Maine Women's Amateur golf tournament, starting when she was just 15. She had been competing for state titles when she was a pre-teen against some of the state's best women golfers. When she was 14, her father reportedly lied about her age to enter her in tournaments all over the East Coast just to see how she would perform.

Spector was born October 16, 1980, in Bristol, Connecticut, but the family moved to Maine when she was tiny. She started playing when her dad worked as greenskeeper in Greenville. He sawed off some clubs for her when she was four, while she was following him on his rounds. Her passion was inflamed immediately. Then her family moved to Waterville to be near the hospital where her mother received cancer treatment, but her mother died when she was nine.

Although Spector took lessons and played in tournaments, she couldn't find many girls playing in the junior leagues, so she played in boys' leagues. A 1999 graduate of Waterville High, she won the high school state girls' golf championship four times from 1995 through 1998, and an American Jr. Golf Association All-American Honorable Mention, and in 1998 she was PGA/Maine State Golf Association player of the year.

She led Waterville to the state Class A golf team championship in 1997. She was Most Valuable Player for both the girls' and boys' teams and chosen for the girls' All-State teams for four years and the boys' for two. She also lettered in indoor track, was elected president of the student council, and earned membership in the National Honor Society.

Upon graduation, she headed for the University of North Carolina on a Division 1 full golf scholarship, studying communications, where she was voted top freshman in 2000. In 2001, she won the New England Women's Amateur title. In 2003, she was "best overall" for the Tar Heels at UNC in 2003. She enjoyed six top-10 finishes at UNC and 14 top-30 finishes. Clearly, she was poised to achieve her dream of being a serious contender on the professional women's tour.

However, in 2003, Spector was diagnosed with a congenital heart defect. She'd had it all her life, but it had been undiscovered. She underwent emergency open heart surgery, but there were complications and she nearly lost her life. She did lose her sight, some of her memory, and her coordination—making hitting a golf ball nearly impossible.

But her indomitable spirit helped with a long, challenging recovery. Her sight returned, as did her coordination. She could once again hit a golf ball, although her career as a professional competitor ended.

She turned pro in 2006 and stayed in the game as an instructor, first at the junior program at Val Halla Golf Course in Cumberland. In 2007, she became the assistant pro at the Gasparilla Inn and Club in Boca Raton, Florida. Summers, she worked at various courses in Maine and New Hampshire.

In 2012, she became the first female golf pro at the Sugarloaf Golf Club in Carrabassett Valley. In 2016, she was hired as head pro at Riverside Golf Course in Portland to run the junior golf program, adult clinics, and to teach private and group lessons.

Spector has an award named for her that is given by the Women's Maine State Golf Association for a lifetime of outstanding golf achievement on and off the course. In 2007, she was inducted into the Maine Golf Hall of Fame, and in 2014 the Maine Sports Hall of Fame.

40

CLYDE SUKEFORTH

Big League Player, Coach, Manager, and the
Guy Who Signed Jackie Robinson

Clyde Leroy "Sukey" Sukeforth was born in Washington, Maine, on November 30, 1901, where he attended the Hodge School, a one-room school (now part of the Matthews Museum in Union). He played baseball as a youngster partly, he said, because "there was nothin' else to do . . . no radio, no TV. . . ." The newspaper arrived from Boston by stagecoach.

His dad also loved playing and was known as a good pitcher. All the neighborhood kids pitched ball every day of the week. The only other activity was digging worms to go fishing.

Sukeforth attended Washington High for two years in a class of four in 1918, then spent a semester at the Oak Grove Seminary in Vassalboro, where he played baseball for the town of Oakland. After that, he finished his last two years of high school and played ball for Coburn Classical Institute in Waterville. Following school, he played for the Great Northern Paper Team in Millinocket for a couple of years.

Georgetown University offered him a scholarship, so he spent two years there playing ball as a left fielder and catcher. In 1926, the Cincinnati Reds signed him and sent the 5-foot, 10-inch, 155-pound catcher to their farm team in Nashua, New Hampshire, the Nashua Millionaires, a Class B New England League Team.

In 1929, the Reds finally played him a lot and it was his best year as a player. Pitching right and batting left, he earned a .354 batting average. Unfortunately for his playing career, he was shot in the right eye while bird hunting, and his eyesight, and therefore his hitting, was greatly impaired. But during the 1931 season just before the accident, he played more than 100 games for the only time in his career.

Traded to the Brooklyn Dodgers in 1932, he was a backup catcher for the next three years, then sent to manage the Montreal Royals, a Dodgers farm team. In 1943, the Dodgers made him a coach. In 1945 at age 43, he had one more year of playing ball when the war created a shortage of men. After a six-year absence from the game, he was sent in as catcher, starting in 13 games. He earned a batting average of .294 in 18 games, for a lifetime average of .264.

But 1945 was a fateful year in other ways. The Dodgers sent Sukeforth to scout the Negro League, to check out a potential player named Jackie Robinson. Although another scout had spotted Robinson, Dodger president Branch Rickey wanted Sukeforth's opinion. Sukeforth recommended him and brought Robinson to Brooklyn for a meeting with Rickey, where the historic signing took place, breaking the color line—the "gentleman's agreement" to keep professional baseball white.

In a sort of fluke, Sukeforth happened to be filling in as unwilling manager of the Dodgers after Leo Durocher's suspension, so he was there to write Robinson's name into the Dodger's lineup when Robinson played his first game at Ebbets Field. They beat the Boston Braves 5–3.

Robinson always credited him with a more important role in integrating baseball than the self-effacing Sukeforth usually received or would accept. Robinson wrote a letter to Sukeforth near the end of his life, saying ". . . there has not been enough said of your significant contribution in the Rickey-Robinson experiment, I consider your role, next to Mr. Rickey's and my wife's—bigger than any other person with whom I came in contact. I have always considered you to be one of the true giants in this initial endeavor in baseball, for which I am truly appreciative."

Sukeforth always downplayed his role, saying he just happened to be in the right place at the right time, but he was well-known to have been a good friend and confidante to Robinson and other black players on and off the field.

He served as a scout for the team from 1936 to 1951, and later for the Pittsburgh Pirates and the Atlanta Braves. Sukeforth helped sign Roberto Clemente to the Dodgers, and was instrumental in bringing Roy Campanella and Don Newcombe into the majors.

"I've only done two things in my life: baseball and chopping wood," Sukeforth told a writer in 2000. He always returned to Maine in the off-season to his 100-acre blueberry and Christmas tree farm in Waldoboro. He loved winter and being outdoors. When he retired from baseball, he moved back to Maine permanently, spending the last 30 years or so in a cabin on the water in Waldoboro. He died at age 98 on September 3, 2000.

He once told a writer, "I don't ask a lot out of life, but I do want contentment. I could never find it as a manager. I have a happy home life, own a farm in Waldoboro, Maine, and among other things I grow there are Christmas trees. It doesn't get any better than that."

Norman Rockwell included Sukeforth in his painting "Bottom of the Sixth." Ken Burns interviewed him for his 1994 documentary "Baseball." The 2013 sports movie about Jackie Robinson breaking the color barrier called "42" includes Sukeforth's character played by actor Toby Huss.

Sukeforth was inducted into the Georgetown Athletic Hall of Fame, the Maine Baseball Hall of Fame in 1969, the Maine Sports Hall of Fame in 1977, and the Midcoast Sports Hall of Fame in 2007. Waldoboro's Prescott Memorial School named its field after him.

Reportedly, there is always a fresh baseball to be found, sitting on his grave.

BILLY SWIFT

Olympian and Major League Pitcher

William Charles "Billy" Swift was the fourteenth of fifteen children in his family. Born in Portland, October 27, 1961, he grew up in South Portland and went to South Portland High School, where he played outfield for the school team.

Swift's father, a former left-handed pitcher for the Portland Pilots, a Class B farm team for the Philadelphia Phillies, named him William for the legendary Red Sox batter, Ted Williams. Swift credits his father for teaching him to throw his best pitch, the sinking fast ball.

From 1981 to 1984, the right-handed Swift played for the Black Bears at the University of Maine in Orono, where he lettered all four years. Starting as an outfielder, he switched to pitching in his sophomore year. For his last two years, he won All-American honors and during 1982–1984 he was chosen for the Eastern College Athletic Conference (ECAC) North All-Conference team.

The Black Bears played in four consecutive NCAA Division I College World Series and finished third in the 1983 series. That year he was drafted in the second round by the Minnesota Twins, but decided to finish his education degree at the University of Maine. He graduated in 1984, when he was the second choice first-round pick of the Seattle Mariners.

When the Olympic Games were held in Los Angeles in 1984, he was the flag-bearer during opening ceremonies. The team took the silver medal, with Swift pitching the winning game against Nicaragua. He also played with the U.S. team in the 1982 World Games in Seoul where they took bronze, the 1983 Pan American Games in Caracas where they won bronze, and the 1983 Intercontinental Cup in Brussels where they won silver.

He signed with the Mariners after the Olympics and pitched in the major leagues for 13 years and three teams. In his first appearance for the Mariners, he came in as a relief pitcher and threw a shutout for five innings.

Early in his career with the Mariners, manager Chuck Cottier said of Swift: "He comes from a family of 15, so there's not much that shakes him up. He's such a nice, quiet, self-controlled kid."

Swift served as a starting pitcher and a relief pitcher, between injuries. In 1989, he was in the middle of pitching a 16-inning scoreless streak when he was beaned by a line drive that fortunately didn't kill him or end his career.

Swift won 40 games in his years with Seattle. In 1991 he enjoyed a successful season as a relief pitcher, fourth in the American League with 71 appearances and a 1.99 ERA for the year. He had the highest groundball/fly ratio of his career at 2.39. Surprisingly, after such a great season, he was traded to the San Francisco Giants along with a few other Mariners.

Swift moved to San Francisco in 1992 where he claimed a 10–4 record. The next year his record was 21–8 and he was a runner-up for the Cy Young award. He set a club record of 21 hits in 80 at-bats, and joined National League leaders in a variety of pitching categories, including third in wins and fourth in ERAs.

From the Giants, he was traded to the Colorado Rockies in 1995 for three seasons, returned to the Giants for one more season and retired in 1998, after struggling for several years with shoulder injuries and back pains.

In 2001, Swift joined the Scottsdale (Arizona) Christian Academy as baseball coach, leading them to four Metro League championships and appearances in 10 state playoff tournaments. In 2013 he moved to Arizona Christian University as head coach achieving 89 wins, the most in the school's history. He resigned in May of 2018.

In 1984 he was named Maine Sports Hall of Fame Scholar Athlete, and in 1994 Swift was inducted into the Maine Sports Hall of Fame. In 1991 he was inducted into the University of Maine Sports Hall of Fame. At the time of his induction into the Maine Baseball Hall of Fame in 2000, he was Maine's winningest major league pitcher. There he joined his father, Herb, who was inducted in 1976. Swift was elected to the New England Baseball Hall of Fame, Springfield, Massachusetts, in 2014.

"I'm a Mainer. I don't have a lot to say about myself," Swift once told a San Francisco reporter, "I mean, I'm not a rah-rah guy yelling in the locker room."

42

FRED TOOTELL

Hammer Thrower, First "Polar Bear" to
Win Olympic Gold

If Fred Tootell hadn't attended Bowdoin College, he might never have been a gold-medal Olympic hammer thrower. And the University of Rhode Island might never have become a powerhouse in the sport.

Born in Lawrence, Massachusetts, on September 9, 1902, Frederick Delmont "Fred" Tootell was one of those multitalented athletes. He enrolled at Bowdoin College where he became an All-Maine and All-New England football player, while also starring on the track and field team, particularly as a 100-meter sprinter.

His track coach, Jack Magee, was legendary at Bowdoin, and he was the first to encourage Tootell to try throwing the hammer. He quickly showed an amazing aptitude for it. When Tootell was a senior, he won the national collegiate championship with a throw of 175 feet, 1 inch. For 40 years, one of his college throws, 185 feet, was the record at Bowdoin as well as a world record.

When he graduated in 1923 as a pre-med and language major, Tootell said he wanted to be a coach and enter the 1924 Olympics. In order to maintain his amateur status, he briefly enrolled in medical school at Tufts University rather than take a job right away. He not only entered the "Chariots of Fire" Paris Olympics as a member of the U.S. Olympic track and field team, but he won gold with a throw of 174 feet, 10⅛ inches.

He accomplished this despite a leg injury that kept him in a cast until the morning of the competition.

He was the first American-born winner of the Olympic hammer throw. The previous five winners for the U.S. Olympic team were all born in Ireland. Tootell was the first Bowdoin Polar Bear and the first Maine athlete to win Olympic gold.

Prior to winning Olympic gold, in his senior year at Bowdoin, he entered the prestigious Penn Relays for the only time, but it was memorable. He set a record for Penn Relays Carnival with a 174-foot, 5-inch throw, a record that remained until 1940. That record made him the seventh longest-throwing athlete in the world at the time.

In 1924, on his way back by train from the Paris Olympics, Tootell accepted an invitation from Frank Keaney, the athletic director for Rhode Island College, later the University of Rhode Island. Tootell disembarked the train at Kingston to have supper with Keaney and began what some writers have called the tiny state's "love affair with the hammer."

Soon after, Tootell became a coach in Rhode Island where he spent 37 years coaching not only track and field, but served as assistant freshman football coach for 22 years, tennis coach for six years, professor of physical education for men for 29 years, and director of athletics and chairman of the Department of Physical Education for men for nine years, assistant freshman football coach for 22 years, tennis coach for six years, professor of physical education for men for 29 years, and director of athletics and chairman of the Department of Physical Education for men for nine years.

Prior to Rhode Island, he spent a short stint coaching and teaching at Mercersburg (Pennsylvania) Academy. In one year, he threw the hammer more than 200 feet six times, the first person ever to break the 200-foot barrier. Because he was working as a coach, he was no longer eligible to compete in international amateur events.

But it was as track and field coach in Rhode Island where he put the tiny state's teams on the map. Under his tutelage, the track and field team won 12 New England intercollegiate titles as well as the National Intercollegiate Championship in 1941. They were undefeated from 1930 to 1937, and had a 99–28–1 record overall. Those records include an unprecedented record of 18 undefeated seasons in cross-country and 17 undefeated seasons in track. He also coached the U.S. team for field events at the Berlin Olympics.

Rhode Island became one of few states to compete and dominate in hammer-throwing at the collegiate level because Tootell started the program. He coached many who became Olympians, many All-Americans, and many who became coaches who spread the popularity of hammer-throwing. He died on September 29, 1964, the same day he retired from the University of Rhode Island. Tootell lived the last 40 years of his life in Kingston, Rhode Island, and had five children.

In his lifetime he served as president of the Association of Collegiate Track Coaches of America, on the National Track Coaches Association, the National Collegiate Cross Country Coaches Association, chairman of the National Collegiate Athletic Association, the IC4A, and the National Amateur Athletic Association (AAU) Track and Rules Committees, member of the Board of Governors of the National AAU, the College Athletic Business Managers Association, National Tennis Coaches Association, and the International Track Coaches Association.

Tootell has been honored many times. The University of Rhode Island's physical education center is named for him. His former home in Kingston, the Tootell House, is on the National Register of Historic Places. The most outstanding field performer at the Maine State Collegiate Track and Field meet receives an award named for him. He was inducted into the Maine Sports Hall of Fame in 1978, the University of Rhode Island Hall of Fame in 1972, the Bowdoin College Athletic Hall of Honor in 2005, and the Penn Relays Carnival Wall of Fame in 2017.

43

SHAWN WALSH

Father of Maine Hockey

The "Father of Maine Hockey" wasn't born in Maine, but he died there at a too-early age. In his extraordinary 16-year tenure at the University of Maine, Shawn Walsh skyrocketed the Black Bears to their first national hockey titles and himself to national coach of the year.

His time at the University of Maine was also marred by his suspension without pay by the university for a year in 1995–1996 after NCAA investigations found he violated National Collegiate Athletic Association (NCAA) rules. The violations included accepting supplemental income from hockey program boosters, playing ineligible students, illegally contacting potential NCAA investigation interviewees, allowing players to accept rent discounts, and promises of player stipends for participation on Olympic teams. The team was also suspended from playoffs for two years.

William Shawn Walsh was born in White Plains, New York, June 21, 1955, where he learned to skate as a small child and fell in love with hockey early on. In high school he played goalie, and again as a third-string goalie at Bowling Green University in Ohio, where, as only a sophomore, he developed an interest in coaching. He coached at Bowling Green, where he also earned his bachelor's and master's in education, and later coached at Michigan State.

But in 1984, he won his first head coaching job at the University of Maine at Orono (UMO), and there he hit his stride and found his home. His first two years, the program had a record of 13–59–2, but Walsh was busy recruiting top players and promoting the program. By 1986, the Bears had their first winning season with Walsh, 24–16–2, even making it into the NCAA tournament. Ironically, UMO lost the first round to Walsh's former employer, Michigan State.

In 1987 and 1988, the Black Bears were conference runner-ups. In 1988–1989, the team beat Boston College by 5–4, winning their first of five Hockey East Association championships (four with Walsh). A testimony to the popularity Walsh brought to the Bears—in 1992, UMO's Alfond Arena added 1,200 seats, bringing capacity above 5,000. That same year, the team was expected to win its first championship, but again lost to Michigan State in the first round.

Things changed dramatically in the 1992–1993 season. A few key Bears players had graduated, and the fairly young team wasn't expected to accomplish much. But the youngsters had a surprise in store for everyone. One remaining star senior, Jim Montgomery, was already UMO's all-time high scorer. He finished his college career with 301 points. The younger stars-to-be made similarly impressive contributions and the Bears ended their regular season with an astonishing 42–1–1.

At the Frozen Four semifinals, a bad call by a referee nearly ended UMO's chances. A good goal that was disallowed caused UMO and the University of Michigan to be tied at the end of regular play. However, the Bears overcame the bad luck with a goal in overtime that won the game. Although the championship game against the Lake Superior State University Lakers was tough and Maine was down 4–2 at the end of second period, Montgomery scored a hat trick in the third, assisted by Paul Kariya on all three goals. Canadian native Kariya later went to the NHL for 15 seasons. The Bears won, 5–4.

In the 1990s, the NCAA spent 18 months investigating college teams who used ineligible players, forcing many teams including UMO to forfeit games retroactively. UMO was allowed to retain the national win because the scoring players were eligible and the questionable players hailed from past teams. UMO dropped three scholarships over two years as a result of the investigation, and didn't participate in any post-season games in 1996 or 1997.

Walsh's suspension and UMO being barred from post-season play meant other colleges tried to poach the Bears' top players. But none of them left, professing loyalty to the coach that brought them the championship, citing his loyalty to them. Walsh had refused many offers to leave UMO for bigger schools and had closely monitored his players' school work as well as their ice time.

Although they were not allowed to skate in any championship games, when Walsh returned to coaching the Bears for the 1996–1997 season, his team ended third in Hockey East with a 15–3–0 record. In 1997–1998, the Bears were Hockey East sixth runner-ups with a 17–5–4 overall record, and 10–11–3 for the conference.

Then came the next big thing: the 1998–1999 season. Walsh was back in stride, the ban on championship games was lifted, and the Bears ended with a conference score of 17–5–2. Although they did not win the conference or even make it to the final, because of a good season, they advanced on an at-large basis to the Frozen Four, where they faced the Boston College team that had knocked them out in the semifinals 3–2. This time the roles were reversed. Maine beat Boston College in overtime, 2–1.

In the final game, Maine faced the neighboring New Hampshire Wildcats, ranked number one in the contest, and who were fast becoming serious, feuding rivals of the Bears. At the end of regulation play, the fast and furious game marked by outstanding Maine goal-tending by conference MVP Alfie Michaud, was tied 2–2. After a breathtaking 10 minutes in overtime, the Bears grabbed the puck, fed it to Marcus Gustafsson who scored the winning goal for UMO's second national championship. Some sports writers have called this team the best NCAA championship team ever.

For a little symmetry and myth-making, this team boasted Steve Kariya, the younger brother of Paul Kariya, who went on to the Canucks and a series of European teams before becoming a coach.

"It's been a wonderful journey," Walsh said after the game. "These guys had faith, loyalty, fraternity, and confidence. The first win in '93 was for the state of Maine. This one is for the players."

Walsh is credited not only with excellent coaching and team-building, but with ginning up the fan base. He created "Maine-iak" shirts that students wore to games. He was known to jump on tables in the university's dining halls to incite the student body to attend games, and then to cheer loudly while there.

Not long after his second big national win, Walsh was diagnosed with renal cell carcinoma, a form of kidney cancer. He died in Bangor, September 24, 2001, at age 46. He was inducted into the University of Maine Sports Hall of Fame in 2002 and in 2003, the Maine Sports Hall of Fame.

He is credited with, in addition to his two national wins, bringing 11 teams to the NCAA tournament, making him fourth for tournament appearances. He brought seven to the Frozen Four, making him the coach who ranks seventh for appearances. Walsh is also credited with the fourth best record of NCAA tournament victories with 20. His 1993 team's season is one of the best in college hockey history. In the 1999 championship game, the two teams took 83 shots, the third most in any championship game history.

Walsh launched the careers of 35 National Hockey League players, coached two Hobey Baker Award winners, 28 All-Americans, eight U.S. Olympians, and two Canadian Olympians. He was awarded the national Spencer Penrose Award for 1994–1995 by the American Hockey Coaches Association, as the top coach in the NCAA division. He took home the Bob Kullen Coach of the Year Award as best coach in the Hockey East/New England conference, four times. Walsh was the winning coach, chosen by the head coaches of each conference team, for 1987–1988, 1989–1990, 1992–1993, and 1994–1995. He was a member of the American Hockey Coaches Association for 10 years and also served as president.

Walsh had five children from two marriages. Following in his father's footsteps, Walsh's son Tyler, a 2014 UMO graduate, was named assistant hockey coach for Colby College in 2018.

When Walsh died, UMO men's basketball coach, John Giannini, said, "I feel like we lost our leader . . . there's no doubt he was our captain (among all UMO sports coaches). It's not even because of coaching success either. It's been more because of his personality and his intellect. He's a very passionate and intelligent person."

44

ERIC WEINRICH

All-America Defenseman, Olympian, and NHL Player

Eric Weinrich was born in Roanoke, Virginia, December 19, 1966, but grew up in Gardiner and went to high school at North Yarmouth Academy (NYA), where he played varsity soccer, hockey, and baseball all four years.

He won Class C State Championships in soccer in his junior and senior years, ending with a career record of 57 wins and 19 losses. His baseball team finished over .500. But hockey was his best game.

In freshman year, and for every year after that, Heinrich was an All-State selection. Sophomore year, he was also chosen for the All New England Prep School All-Star Team. Junior year, he was again on the All-Star prep school team and third in the league in scoring. Senior year, he was All-State and All-New England again, as well as Minor Hockey League All-Conference First Team.

Weinrich led his NYA team to its first Class A State Championship ending with a 60–19 overall record. He graduated in 1985.

While still a student at NYA, he started playing for the U.S. Junior National Team during the 1984–1985 season. He then enrolled at the University of Maine in Orono (UMO) to study archeology and anthropology, but continued skating in the international events as well as for the UMO Black Bears, until his senior year when he joined the U.S.

Olympic team. All told, he played in nine world championships for Team USA, the most of any American-born player.

Weinrich was named an NCAA East Second Team All-American, as well as winning All-Hockey East and All-New England honors in the 1986–1987 season. He was a member of the first two Black Bears hockey teams to make it into the NCAA Tournament coached by the team's legendary Shawn Walsh. He played 83 games in three seasons with the Black Bears.

He was scouted by the pros starting in high school. The Buffalo Sabres wanted him in 1984, but he was too young. In 1985, he was drafted by the National Hockey League's (NHL) New Jersey Devils, joined their American Hockey League (AHL) Utica Devils for two seasons starting in 1988. In 1990, he was honored with the Eddie Shore Award for the player chosen by the AHL coaches, media, and players as the best defenseman in the league.

Weinrich also played 21 games for the NHL Devils during those AHL years, joining the team full-time in 1990, his best year. He scored 38 points and was chosen for the NHL All-Rookie Team. He went on to play for the Hartford Whalers, Chicago Blackhawks, Montreal Canadiens, Boston Bruins, Philadelphia Flyers, St. Louis Blues, and Vancouver Canucks during his 17 seasons in the NHL.

During the 2004–2005 NHL lockout, Weinrich went to Austria to play for the VSV EC in the Austrian Hockey League, before rejoining the St. Louis Blues. He played a total 1,157 NHL games, scored 70 goals and 318 assists, earning 388 points.

He announced his retirement in 2006, signing on as an assistant coach for Maine's Portland Pirates. However, some months later, he signed on to become an active defenseman for the Pirates and played 36 games, scoring two goals and adding 14 points. Before he left the Pirates in 2008, he was the oldest active player in the AHL at age 40.

Weinrich worked as professional scout for the Buffalo Sabres for three years, then became a development coach for the New Jersey Devils. In 2016, he and his wife, Tracy, and their two children, moved to a home on Cousins Island, Maine.

One writer said Weinrich is one of Maine's top athletes, ever, and not nearly well enough appreciated: "He has merely played one of the most thankless positions in professional sports without fanfare or complaint for eight different franchises. . . . He has maintained said value without flaunting otherworldly offensive talent and without devolving into a belligerent thug. Basically, he was everything we collectively cried that professional sports should be."

Weinrich was inducted into the University of Maine Sports Hall of Fame in 1994 and the Maine Sports Hall of Fame in 2015. In 1988, he had been given a special achievement award by the Maine Sports Hall of Fame. In 2016, he was inducted into the North Yarmouth Academy Edgar F. White '38 Athletic Hall of Fame. In 2015, he joined Bill Guerin as an honorary captain for the AHL All-Star Classic in Utica, New York, an honor that recognizes former players for their careers.

45

COLEY WELCH

The Fighting Iceman

Coleman Patrick "Coley" Welch was like many fighters, a scrappy young man in the Depression when jobs were scarce and poorly paid outdoor boxing matches were frequent.

Born February 8, 1919, in Portland, Welch began his career in 1936 as a lightweight amateur who trained in a warehouse where coffins were made, "in an era of what they call hungry fighters," said his brother, Paul. He lost both parents before he was eight, so he spent some early years with an aunt in South Boston, but returned to Portland for high school.

His first professional fight took place in 1936 at the Portland Expo when he was 18, and Welch continued to fight throughout New England and in New York for the next 13 years. The Expo opened in 1915. Before that, Portland fighters fought outdoors in clandestine wooded spots, often in Cape Elizabeth.

The 5-foot, 7-inch, 170-pound "body puncher" became a middleweight and by 1941 was ranked number three in the world by *The Ring* magazine, the boxing bible. Welch, who was the most prominent of Portland's fighters during his career, was known for wearing down his opponents. Welch was always a top draw with boxing fans in his heyday.

He was the New England Middleweight champion for six years until his most famous fight—a loss—in 1944. The luck of the Irish ran out on Welch on St. Patrick's Day in Boston Garden, when The Fighting Iceman faced off against The Raging Bull, Jack LaMotta.

Welch had interrupted his career for a short stint in the Coast Guard, but returned to boxing in 1943, winning 15 straight decisions before the LaMotta fight. LaMotta easily won a unanimous decision against Welch before a crowd of 10,000. But Welch went toe-to-toe with LaMotta for ten rounds.

When the first fight was broadcast on the radio from the Expo in 1940, it was a Welch fight in which he defeated Babe Verila. Before retiring in 1949, Welch fought 117 bouts for a total of 850 rounds. During his impressive career, he racked up 105 wins, 24 losses, and six draws. Fifty-one of his wins were by knockout and four of his losses.

After he retired from boxing, Welch ran a bar on Brackett St. in Portland. Then he moved to Las Vegas in the 1960s where he worked as a security guard, eventually at Caesars Palace. It's reported that Frank Sinatra and other visiting Las Vegas celebrities, such as Joe DiMaggio, remembered Welch from his fights at Madison Square Garden and treated him with great respect.

Welch was well-known in Vegas gyms, which he frequently visited, offering welcome advice to young fighters. He died of congestive heart failure at age 81 on December 4, 2000, in Las Vegas. He never smoked, stayed at his fighting weight, and was healthy until the last year of his life, according to reports. His daughter did say he enjoyed the occasional shot of Irish whiskey. Welch had two daughters and two sons.

He was inducted into the Maine Sports Hall of Fame in 1986.

(46)

SETH WESCOTT

Olympic Gold-Medal Snowboarder

Seth Wescott was born in North Carolina, June 28, 1976, but he moved to Maine with his family when he was only two and began cross-country skiing when he was only three. By eight he was alpine skiing, and at ten he added snowboarding to his repertoire and immediately began competing in both events. The family lived in Farmington, where his parents were college professors.

After three years, Wescott devoted himself strictly to snowboarding events.

It was probably a good decision since he won gold medals in the first two snowboard cross events ever held in the Olympics.

Wescott graduated from Mt. Blue High School in 1994, went to Western State College of Colorado, and returned to Maine to attend Carrabassett Valley Academy, a small private 9-month prep school where studies include skiing and snowboarding. The school has produced 12 Olympians and a raft of other champions since its founding in 1982 at the base of Sugarloaf, Wescott's home mountain. Sugarloaf is 4,237 feet high, Maine's second-highest peak, boasting 2,820 vertical feet for skiing and snowboarding.

By 1996, Wescott was focused on half-pipe events. A year later his interest turned to snowboard cross, aka boarder cross or SBX, events.

He was U.S. national champion in SBX from 2000 to 2003, took silver in SBX at the Winter X games in 2002, and was third overall in the 2002 World Tour for SBX. After he finished tenth in halfpipe in 2003, he stopped competing in that category.

"I like snowboard cross because I get rewarded for what I do," said Wescoff, unlike halfpipe which is a judged, more subjective sport. He blamed judging for his failure to make the U.S. Olympic team in half-pipe in 1998 and 2002,

Also in 2003, Wescott took the silver medal in SBX at the World Championships and the next year at the Winter X games and the World Cup. In 2005, he finished second in SBX at the Winter X Games and won gold at the World Championships.

In SBX, four snowboarders leave a gate to ride down a 3,000-foot course, making jumps and turns as they go. It's fast, highly competitive, and can involve many collisions. During preliminary heats, boarders race the clock until four emerge as finalists. Then the four race against each other for the victory. Wescott lobbied hard for SBX to be included in the Olympics and finally succeeded for the 2006 event.

In 2006, Wescott won the gold medal in SBX in the Winter Olympic Games in Turin, Italy, the first time SBX was featured in the Olympics. He was invited to the White House, but declined the offer because he opposed George W. Bush's foreign and domestic politics.

During the years until the next Olympics, Wescott raced in World Cup events and began a new regimen of training by snowboarding huge mountains in Alaska, the Himalayas, and the Southern Hemisphere.

When the second SBX Olympic event was held at the 2010 games in Vancouver, British Columbia, Wescott took gold once again. He wrapped himself in his grandfather's American flag as a celebration of the win and to honor his grandfather's service during World War II.

He might have repeated his gold at the next Winter Olympics as well, but he fell into a crevasse in 2013, snowboarding in Alaska while filming a documentary. Racing down the big mountains involved being dropped off at the peak by a helicopter and finding his way through unfamiliar terrain. The complete reconstruction of his left ACL meant he couldn't recover in time to qualify for 2014.

In addition to his snowboarding career, Wescott co-owns The Rack, a popular restaurant and brew pub near Sugarloaf, and is an owner and designer for Winterstick, a snowboarding manufacturer. He appeared on the Colbert Report in 2010, and the Fox dating game show The Choice in 2012.

He has served as an ambassador for Take It Outside, a state initiative to reconnect Maine children with nature, as a spokesperson for WinterKids, another effort to interest Maine kids in winter sports, and supported Level Field Fund, a program to provide some funding for young athletes needing financial assistance.

Wescott is one of the most decorated snowboarders in the sport. By 2016, he had 153 X Games medals and 12 World Cup medals: four gold, four silver, and three bronze. He reached the podium five times in Grand Prix competition and was three times national champion and has won awards in every major SBX world event. He was tenth in his last World Cup run in 2017. Wescott was inducted into the Maine Ski and Snowboard Hall of Fame in 2019 in a ceremony held at Sugarloaf.

47

HAROLD "BUD" WHITE

Triple Threat from Auburn

War has interrupted and thereby ended the promising careers of many an athlete, and Harold "Bud" White was one.

White, born in Auburn on May 17, 1917, and raised on Whiteholm Farm with his two brothers and two sisters, was one of those multi-talented athletes. He excelled in the water as a swimmer, and on land as a baseball pitcher and javelin thrower.

His dad was swimming coach for the Auburn YMCA in the early 1930s, so White began swimming for his father as a youngster. When he attended Edward Little High School in Auburn, he competed as a swimmer for all four years and set records for 40, 50, and 100 yards in the freestyle. He remained undefeated in individual dual competition events, and his state records set in 1935 were unbroken for six years. He earned high school All-American status and was twice named the state's top swimmer. He was also a star pitcher on the baseball team.

White went on to Bowdoin College in Brunswick where he joined the swim team and the baseball team. As a swimmer, he continued his undefeated status as a freestyle sprinter for his entire college career. He captained the swim team, was a five-time New England Champion, became New England College Swimmer of the Year in 1938, and also became the first Bowdoin All-American swimmer.

Once again, he became a record-holder, this time in the 50, 60, and 100 events in 1937, 1938, and 1939. His coach felt he would be a top contender for the 1940 Tokyo Olympic games, but they were canceled.

When he wasn't swimming, he was pitching. He pitched the Polar Bears to the state championship in 1936 and 1938, winning All-State honors in 1938 and 1939. He lettered all four years. During his college career, he won a total of nine varsity letters.

Legendary Bowdoin track and field coach Jack Magee enticed White to try throwing the javelin. Without practice, he threw it 186 feet, 1½ inches and won the 1938 state meet. He lettered in the javelin throw in 1938 and 1939. Sometimes White would pitch for the baseball team, and when the game was over, head to the track field to throw the javelin.

He was a powerful player, nearly 6 feet, 4 inches, and more than 200 pounds, and it appeared as though baseball would be his career. The Red Sox sought him out upon graduation in 1939. When he visited the Red Sox for tryouts, he roomed and practiced with Ted Williams. Boston's legendary hitter would tell White to put his fastball right down the middle, and in one week of practice, Williams never hit that fast ball.

His brother said Bud's fast ball was never timed, but it was rumored to fly at about 120 miles per hour. White played for three years with Boston farm teams, posting a 38–19 record. He was given a contract with the Louisville team, based on his 1941 record, 21–6 with the Oneonta, New York, team. His future at Fenway looked bright.

But World War II came along. White spent four years in the army and never got back to playing professional baseball. He didn't leave the sport altogether, however. He became a baseball coach and athletic director for Thornton Academy in Saco.

In a strange historical quirk, White had a son named for him, Harold "Bud" White III, who was a football and baseball player and a swimmer. After attending Rutgers, he spent two promising seasons in the Baltimore Orioles farm system, when he was sent to Vietnam, ending his baseball career. White also had another son and a daughter. He died in 1992.

White was inducted into the Maine Sports Hall of Fame in 1983, the Lewiston-Auburn Sports Hall of Fame in 1985, the Maine Swimming and Diving Hall of Fame in 2008, and the Bowdoin College Athletic Hall of Honor in 2009.

His biography for the Bowdoin Hall of Honor says, "A member of Bowdoin's astonishing class of 1939, Harold "Bud" White Jr. was not only one of the finest all-around athletes to perform beneath the pines, but he was also one of the finest of his era in intercollegiate competition."

48

CARLTON WILLEY

The Star That Might Have Been

History turns on unexpected incidents. Who knows if Carlton Willey would have continued playing and had a spectacular career if his jaw hadn't been broken by a baseball during spring training in 1964?

Carlton Francis Willey was born June 6, 1931, in Cherryfield, a small town Downeast. When he played baseball in a field with his playmates, they used rocks as bases. At the public Cherryfield Academy, he pitched and played right field for his tiny team.

At a tryout in Bangor for the Boston Braves, Willey landed a spot on the team's Bangor club, one of four they had in Maine. At the end of the summer, he went to Boston for another tryout and impressed the managers with his fast ball. He was signed to a contract immediately.

He was called into the army for two years in 1953, which he said set him back four years in baseball, because it took two more years to get back in shape.

The 6-foot, 175-pound right-handed pitcher spent the next few years in the Braves' AAA teams from Quebec to Atlanta, winning the (now defunct) American Association Most Valuable Player Award in 1957 for the best player in the minor league that year, playing for the Wichita Aeros.

He led the league with 247 innings pitched, 21 games won, struck out 174 batters, and walked 94. This award was given out from 1929 through 1997.

When he went to pitch for the Braves (by that time in Milwaukee) in 1958, he was named National League Rookie of the Year by *Sporting News*. It was the best year of his eight in major league baseball. Willey earned a 9–7 record for the Braves—a team that was not short on good pitchers already—pitched four shutouts, and helped them win the pennant. One of his shutouts occurred in his first game for the Braves. He also boasted a 2.70 ERA.

The Braves played the Yankees in the World Series and the rookie pitched one scoreless inning for his team, and although the Braves enjoyed a 3–1 lead, they ended up losing the series.

Willey played five seasons for the Braves before moving to the New York Mets. He asked to be traded because the strength of the Braves pitching lineup meant he had few opportunities to play, despite his impressive first year.

In 1963, the team's second year in the league, he joined the Mets. Although a former teammate said the team was bad in 1963 with a weak defense, Willey started 28 games, struck out 101 batters, and won nine of the 51 wins the Mets had. He threw seven complete games and four shutouts. He had few home runs in his career, but one of them was a grand slam in July of 1963.

That year Willey accomplished another feat for the record books: He retired the side in September during a game against the New York Giants, that included all three Alou brothers—Jesus, Matty, and Felipe batting consecutively for the first time. A major league first and only. The Mets won 4–2.

Willey loved the Mets and was poised to become the team's star, but after a strong spring training in 1964, just before the regular season began, he was hit in the jaw by a line drive and suffered a complex compound fracture. He was on the disabled list for two months, but after three game starts, he developed a sore arm. He pitched only two innings for the rest of the season. Constant pain hampered his abilities and a wired jaw meant he couldn't eat enough to keep up his strength.

The next year was similar. Although he started 13 games, his performance was mediocre, so he decided to pack it in. He ended his career with an ERA of 3.76 and 493 strikeouts.

For much of the next decade he scouted for the Philadelphia Phillies, but tired of the travel and went home to Cherryfield to spend time with his son and daughter.

After baseball, he did a variety of jobs in Maine including managing a blueberry freezing plant, working as a probation/parole officer for the state, and raising Christmas trees.

When asked why he returned to Cherryfield, he said, "This is home, I guess. It's hard to get away from."

Although all reports credit Willey with being well-loved by everyone who knew him, one local resident said he wasn't perfect—because he was a Yankees fan in Red Sox Nation.

On July 20, 2009, Willey died of lung cancer in a hospital in nearby Ellsworth at age 78. He was inducted into the Maine Baseball Hall of Fame in 1970 and the Maine Sports Hall of Fame in 1984.

49

GARY WILLIAMSON

MVP, First National Championship Team from Maine

Gary Williamson was born and raised in Bethel, a small town snuggled in the mountains near the New Hampshire border, better-known for skiing than baseball.

Williamson attended the local Telstar High School where he and a group of competitive baseball-playing friends and classmates took the Telstar Rebels to the Western Class C regional championships in 1988 and won. Then they did it again in 1989.

He was recruited for St. Joseph's College in Standish by a pair of coaches who left to work at the University of Southern Maine (USM) after one season, so Williamson followed.

In 1991, the USM Huskies went to the college World Series. The team made the series because of a playoff game against Eastern Connecticut in which Williamson came to bat in the ninth inning with the game tied.

Bases were loaded and there were two outs. Williamson whacked the ball over the left field wall for the biggest home run in USM history. The win took the Huskies to the championship game. Williamson was always known for big home runs, often smashing the ball out of the park over the tops of tall trees.

The Division III College World Series was held in Battle Creek, Michigan, in 1991. After their playoff win, USM played Trenton State College for the title. The Huskies won 9-0 for the first national championship won by a Maine team. Williamson was named NCAA Regional MVP and World Series MVP.

His college batting average of 379 ranks 15th in USM records, and his 26 home runs place him fifth.

Williamson never pursued a professional career. He joined the Pine Tree League, playing with a diverse group of 18–50-year olds of varying backgrounds—everything from high school kids to former professionals. It's a summer, wooden-bat league played just for fun.

He met his wife, Julia, at USM. They have four sons. Williamson launched a career selling real estate in the Bethel area. He began coaching little kids, including his boys, and found he had a passion for it. "One thing I can tell you about coaching, young kids learn it just as quick as college kids. It's just how you go about it."

In 2016, Williamson was inducted into the Maine Baseball Hall of Fame. His former USM coach, Ed Flaherty, also a Hall of Fame member, said, "Gary played the game the way it should be played. He was a fearless competitor. . . . He was ultra-aggressive with the bat and the way he ran the bases. He made others around him better because of the aggressiveness he played with."

JOHN WINKIN

Baseball Coach Extraordinaire for Colby,
University of Maine, and Husson

He might have been born and raised in New Jersey, but once John Winkin adopted Maine as home, he never left. Winkin's mother was a doctor at Columbia Presbyterian Medical College and his father a Columbia University linguistics professor. Winkin was not supposed to become a baseball coach.

Born in Englewood, July 24, 1919, John W. Winkin Jr. started out on a more expected path, although he did play football, baseball, and basketball in high school. While studying education at Duke University, he played baseball, where his coach was "Colby Jack" Coombs, a harbinger of Winkin's future. In fact, the 5-foot, 6-inch, 150-pound left-handed center fielder also played basketball and soccer and lettered in all three sports before graduating in 1941.

After college, Winkin joined the Navy where he narrowly avoided death when his ship, the USS *McCall*, was delayed by hazardous weather, otherwise it would have been berthed next to the USS *Arizona* at Pearl Harbor when it was bombed by the Japanese.

Following his discharge four and half years later, Winkin returned to New Jersey, where he did not heed coach Coombs's advice and go into coaching, because he knew his parents wouldn't approve. Instead, he took up sports journalism, helped start *SPORT Magazine* and was an early TV sports analyst for the Yankees. He also managed to sneak in a little coaching by managing the American Legion baseball team in his hometown.

The hook was set. In 1949, he started coaching football and baseball at an Englewood high school while also teaching history. Meanwhile, he pleased his parents by earning a masters and doctorate in education at Columbia, using the statistical probabilities of the double play as his doctoral thesis.

By 1954, the pretense was over. Coombs recommended Wilkin for a coaching position at his alma mater, Colby. Wilkin spent the next 20 years as Colby's baseball coach and athletic director. During his tenure he also served as president of the Eastern College Athletic Conference (ECAC) and vice president of the National Collegiate Athletic Association (NCAA). In 1965, he was named National Baseball Coach of the Year. He counted for the Boston Red Sox, became friends with Ted Williams, and coached summers at Williams's youth baseball camps.

His teams won 13 Maine state titles and one New England championship. Over his career, his record was 301–202–5. His last year, he also served as president of the National Association of Collegiate Directors of Athletics.

In 1975, Winkin went on to the University of Maine at Orono, bringing the Black Bears to new heights that included competing in six college World Series, taking one third place, and finishing in the top three twice. His wins surprised everyone since his players were drawn mostly from Maine and New England. The Black Bears were forced to compete against bigger schools with more money that could scout and attract talent. Add to that the short season for outdoor play in Maine.

Winkin overcame the winter weather obstacles by developing his own program for indoor training, helped by UMO's unusually large field house. When he wrote four books about baseball later, one of them outlined this indoor method, "Maximizing Baseball Practice Indoors." In 1983, he coached the U.S. National Team, which boasted Mark McGwire, later a pro, record-breaking home run hitter.

Before the NCAA changed its rules, making it more difficult for a small, northern school to qualify for the championships, Winkin put Orono on the baseball map. In 1985, the team set a school record for wins, 38–17, including one against powerhouse Miami. In 1986, the

Black Bears set another record, winning more than 40 games (41) for the first time in school history. When he left Orono in 1996, Winkin's coaching record there was 642–430–3.

By this time, he was 77, beyond the age when most people retire. But Winkin accepted another post as an assistant baseball coach the Eagles at Division III Husson University in Bangor, along with a position as fellow for sports and leadership. He became head coach in 2003. At age 86, he became the forty-fourth college coach in the country to achieve 1,000 wins and the oldest working coach in any sport in the NCAA, ever.

Winkin had a stroke in 2007 while taking his daily three-mile walk. He recovered, but with partial paralysis of his right side and wheelchair-bound. He stayed on through 2008 as coach, stepped down at the end of the season, but remained as assistant coach. In his career he totaled 1,043 wins, 52nd among NCAA head coaches. His record at Husson was 100–74–8. He died in a Waterville nursing home on July 19, 2014, at age 94, after living in Maine for 60 years.

All three colleges retired his Number 5 jersey. His coaching career spawned 92 players who signed professional contracts, including Mainers Billy Swift and Bert Roberge. He won many awards and was inducted into 11 halls of fame, including the National College Baseball Hall of Fame in 2013 for his work at all three colleges. Others include: The Maine Sports Hall of Fame, The Husson University Sports Hall of Fame, the American Baseball Coaches Association Hall of Fame (which established an award for Maine high school baseball players in his name), the University of Maine Sports Hall of Fame, and the Maine Baseball Hall of Fame. The Husson baseball facility is named the Dr. John W. Winkin Sports Complex.

His assistant coach for 11 years and former Black Bear, Mike Coutts, said, "You realize the passion that he had for the game, and then you realize how competitive he was and how every time he went out, he made you believe that you can compete with anybody in the country."

"When I became a major league pitcher, I just had that basis and that foundation of what he taught," said Bill Swift, who played for Winkin on the Black Bears from 1981 to 1984. "He gave me the opportunity to play. I couldn't afford college, with 14 brothers and sisters. He really opened the doors for me, just letting me go, inviting me, recruiting me."

AFTERWORD

No One Does It Alone

Athletics in Maine have been helped by many private donors, including the state's most famous resident, horror writer Stephen King. Here are just a few out of many of the generous individuals who have contributed so much to assist Maine's young sports hopefuls to pursue their dreams.

Stephen King lives and breathes baseball. That is, when he isn't creating monsters made famous in his many novels, short stories, and the movies made from them. In 1989, with three other people, the best-selling author helped coach a Bangor 11–12-year-old all-star team that won a state championship and qualified for a regional tournament. The experience led the participants to think about plans for a better field for the kids.

The Stephen and Tabitha King Foundation put $1 million toward the $1.2 million stadium that opened in 1991, and was given to the city of Bangor. The facility was named Mansfield Stadium in honor of Shawn Trevor Mansfield, a son of one of the other coaches of that winning team. Shawn spent his entire life battling cerebral palsy, much of it in a wheelchair. He died at the age of 14. In addition to Little League, the field hosts high school and college teams as well as their state and regional championship games and Bangor's American Legion team. The field boasts top modern engineering to preserve it in excellent condition during Maine's harsh weather seasons. The field is a regulation AA baseball field, locally and affectionately known as the "Field of Screams," located very near the Kings' home with the famous wrought iron fence bedecked with bats and such. The Stephen and Tabitha King Foundation also makes charitable contributions to many other Maine entities, such as libraries.

The Mahaney family boasts three members in several sports halls of fame. Larry Mahaney was a standout athlete in basketball, baseball, and track as a high school student in Fort Fairfield and a 1951 graduate of the University of Maine. He was a successful player and coach. His brother, Keith Mahaney, was also a standout three-sport Fort Fairfield High School athlete who held 11 out of 14 college basketball records before graduating from the University of Maine. Larry's son, Kevin, another standout high school and college athlete, won an Olympic medal in sailing. Larry donated enough money to allow for several renovations to the baseball stadium at the University of Maine (now named Mahaney Diamond), and to build the Mahaney Dome, an indoor practice facility. There's another at St. Joseph's College and a Larry K. Mahaney Gymnasium at Thomas College in Waterville.

The Hadlock family of Maine baseball fame, has two members in the state's baseball hall of fame. Edson B. Hadlock was the Portland High School baseball coach from 1956 to 1978, and was inducted into the Maine Baseball Hall of Fame in 1976. Terry Hadlock, his nephew, and son of semi-pro player, Edmund, was inducted into the Hall of Fame in 1992. Hadlock Field in Portland, the AA baseball field that's home to the Portland Sea Dogs, is named for Edson.

Many sports facilities in Maine bear the name "Alfond." That's because Harold Alfond loved sports and Maine. As with other generous contributors, the Alfond family supports many other charitable causes besides sports. Although he was born in Massachusetts in 1914, where he was an outstanding high school athlete, Harold Alfond migrated to Kennebunk, Maine, following his father into the shoe business. By age 22, he was superintendent of a factory, and in 1940 he and his father bought an abandoned Norridgewock factory where they made mid-priced leather shoes. Four years later they sold it. In 1958, he bought a vacant woolen mill in Dexter and launched Dexter Shoe, a highly profitable and popular shoe line sold in many kinds of stores including their hallmark log cabin stores. He's credited with inventing the factory outlet. In 1993, Alfond sold Dexter to Berkshire Hathaway whose owner, Warren Buffett, called it one of the best-run companies he'd ever seen.

He founded the Harold Alfond Foundation, which gave money to hospitals, health centers, boys' and girls' clubs and colleges, funded scholarships, community centers, and helped displaced shoe workers; plus, Alfond secretly paid school tuitions for many of his employee's children. The foundation contributed millions for sports venues at colleges, often insisting they must also be available for use by their communities. Colby College has the Alfond ice arena and an athletic center. The University of Maine in Orono has a sports stadium, hockey arena, and arena clubhouse. Husson College has a baseball diamond. Thomas College has the athletic center. The Eaglebrook School has an ice arena. In 1996, he also launched Dexter Enterprises, Inc., another philanthropic foundation, which built an 18-hole public golf club in Belgrade Lakes.

Other generous folks have contributed money, time, and expertise to helping athletes in Maine, including such as Carl Soderberg, who has built miles of Nordic ski and mountain bike trails, and ski hills, in Northern Maine. The children, college students, and amateur athletes in Maine have benefited from the philanthropy of these and many others.